BOOK TEN

WORD UNLIMITED
Divinely Maternal

Sylvester L. Steffen

The Book-End to

The EVOLUTION TRILOGIES

— The DIVINICON —

www.divinicom.com

WORD UNLIMITED

Divinely Maternal

Sylvester L Steffen

authorHOUSE®

AuthorHouse™
1663 Liberty Drive
Bloomington, IN 47403
www.authorhouse.com
Phone: 1-800-839-8640

First published by AuthorHouse 11/17/2011
ISBN: 978-1-4670-6458-3 (sc)
ISBN: 978-1-4670-6457-6 (hc)
ISBN: 978-1-4670-6456-9(e)
Library of Congress Control Number: 2011918720
Printed in the United States of America
This book is printed on acid-free paper.

Cover Credits

PIETA Sculpture by Peter Weyland, SVD, 1895-1969
In the Entry to the Mission Chapel,
Divine Word Mission International, TECHNY TOWERS,
2001 Waukegan Road, P.O. Box 176, Techny, IL 60082
www.divineword.org

"MATER EVANGELII PRAECONUM"
"Mother of Heralds of the Gospel"

Photograph by Gerald J. Theis, SVD
Used with permission

S.V.D.
Latin initials for Societas Verbi Divini
English: the Society of the Divine Word
Founded by Saint Arnold Janssen, S.V.D.

Saint Arnold Janssen founded three Religious Orders,
One for men (priests and brothers) and two for women,
One contemplative and one active in mission work.

The

WISDOM

Of

EVOLUTION THEOLOGY

Life supposes death as death supposes life
Old Church must die for New Church to be Reborn

MYSTERY and MYSTICISM
Come to This:

The Process of Spiritual Ascendancy:
Communication-Consciousness-Conscience /
Intelligence

Trinitarian Godlikeness
— DIVINITY CONSCIOUSNESS —

ICONIC TRINITY
WORD-LIGHT-LOVE / WISDOM
The Divine / Human Hypostasis

PREFACE

DIVINITY CONSCIOUSNESS

"Et Verbum Caro Factum Est" — The WORD is Made Flesh

Comes now "WORD UNLIMITED, Divinely Maternal," "Book-End" to the three Evolution Trilogies — The DIVINICON. www. divinicom.com

Bringing to life the Divine WORD is uniquely woman's work, the self-outpouring of body in Godliness. Males talk, but not the Mother language of Word-made-flesh — of "second comings" — what is distinctively woman's work.

"Second Enlightenment" informs the consciousness of "second comings," the vital processes of Divinity Consciousness informing Word and Work — what Eucharist does, is.

Divine/ Human HYPOSTASIS is the ongoing Word/ Work of WISDOM by way of WORD-LIGHT-LOVE — Trinitarian Processing in the SACRAMENT of NATURAL ORDER. Inseparably, life's consecrated order in Sacrament is female/ male.

http://bookstore.authorhouse.com/AdvancedSearch/Default. aspx?SearchTerm=Sylvester%20L%20Steffen

FOREWORD

DESCENT from the CROSS

The heart of Divinity Consciousness is belief in God-Suffering. The iconic image of God-Suffering is Jesus, on the cross, removed from the cross and returned to His Mother's arms — the Beatrix Femina. No one is more intimate in God-Suffering than Woman, the personal ground of Sacred Remembrance.

The mission of every generation is to personalize the consciousness of divine Compassion, which intends the personal renewal of Eucharistic suffering by way of Trimorphic Resonance, the ever refreshed lessons of faith's communication, hope's consciousness and love's conscience.

Doing theology is personal/ social work, everyone's privilege and responsibility. The cumulative havoc of wasted Earth-life weighs not just on humankind but on God-Suffering, and calls for a new sense of doing theology.

The mortal threat to life on Earth highlights the enduring hurt of God-Suffering, and reminds us that, in common, we are all implicated in the Divine Tragedy. We are called to be compassionate even as God is compassionate. Theology renewed, done together, is the communal work of privilege and responsibility.

GODTALK Online

What's new is the way of "doing theology" today. If God is Love's deep impulse inspiring consciousness within, then, we individually are called upon to respond. The dialogue of communication is the response to Call, what is doing theology. In plain talk, doing theology is GOD TALK. Theistic consciousness, the universal instance of Love (divinity) works in nature, in us personally.

As never before, GOD TALK takes place globally and interpersonally at the same time, thanks to postmodern online wave-communication. The inner impulse of communication can now be transmitted more intentionally and at will. This is fortuitous because all can participate ongoing in doing theology. So, let's do it, and get it right — with God, nature and each other.

http://godtalkonline.blogspot.com/2011/08/evolution-theology.html

BLESSED WOMAN

Humankind is in God's likeness, female/ male. Communication at its source is female/ male dialogue, the "vox populi," people together doing theology. GOD TALK is interpersonal communication striving to understand and attain pinnacle perfection, what is understanding what it is to be "Godly." Compulsion to understand and be more Godlike is the inner restlessness of Love, of deep soul inspiration. The pinnacle expression of love is "Eucharist," the deep and intense consciousness and experience of love between mother and child — especially at the critical experience of death.

"Doing Theology" is people-work, the work of love, understanding and striving in response to the ultimate magnetism of Godlikeness. To this all are called, all are destined. Theology is personal, essentially intentional, is religious openness involving the global community in common interests of coming to sustainable Earth/ human accommodation. The "sustainable accommodation" of people with each other and with web-life (ecology) is the precondition of humankind coming to the greater perfection of becoming more Godlike. Honoring Mother Nature, the ground-condition of Earth-life is true religion from which Godlike compassion originates.

FEMININITY, the Ground-State of Vitality

If femininity (femaleness) is the ground-state of vitality, how is it that women are reduced to subserviency in patriarchal culture?

Scholastic Theology, dating back to the 1200s, and to philosophers of earlier times, is the theology of Roman Catholicism, rooted in Abrahamic Tradition. The preeminent apologist of Scholasticism is the revered Saint Thomas Aquinas. Before we treat him too harshly we should acknowledge that his rationality roots in the science of his time and in belief advanced from the Genesis Stories of Creation and Original Sin. Specifically, relying on the credibility of the Genesis account of Eve created from the rib of Adam, the "angelic doctor" argued that woman depends from man and is subservient to him. Evolution science debunks literal credence in the presumption of female derivation from the male sex.

To Thomas Aquinas's credit, toward the end of his life he shut down his writing, believing that what he wrote was so much "straw." Notwithstanding the enlightenment he came to in his later years, Roman Catholicism in practice still preaches the "straw" rationality of early Thomism. Consistent with Vatican II, this writing exposes cultural demeaning and religious alienation that deprive humankind the Eucharistic sensitivity of the Divine Feminine.

INTRODUCTION

Passion, Compassion and Eucharistic Enlightenment

In his book "Redeeming the Enlightenment", 2010 copyright, Wm. B. Eerdman's Publisher, Bruce K. Ward addresses the redemption of Enlightenment by way of attaching Christian sensitivity to the "liberal virtues" of the Enlightenment, most notably the virtues of tolerance and compassion. It might well be observed that religion is in need of Enlightenment as much as Enlightenment needs religion. Enlightenment and religion are so related that one cannot be redeemed except both are. Religion supposes enlightenment as faith supposes reason.

Enlightenment needs religion's trust as religion needs Enlightenment's trust. There can be no meaningful dialog except there is mutual trust. Religion (faith) and Enlightenment (reason) can trust only when each accepts that the other has useful truths to share. Trust realizes that there is truth in differences, and when there is openness to trust, to differences, dialog can open both communicants to new truths. "Compassionate trust" embraces differences, not just "tolerates" them. The problem between Christianity and Enlightenment is analogous to the woman/ nature conundrum pointed out by Walter Brueggemann, that the desecration of nature is unlikely to be remedied (redeemed) except alienation and the desecration of women are remedied at the same time .

http://www.gather.com/viewArticle.action?articleId=2814749775 42405

The significance of this is that the universal premise of evolving consciousness (trustful communication, compassionate tolerance) applies mutually to woman and man, faith and reason, and to religion and enlightenment. The unresolved obstacle to trust is religion's fixation in a worldview (static) that makes no sense to modern understanding; mutually exclusive worldviews inherently distrust each other. Fixation in conflicted worldviews frustrates communication.

What Bruce K. Ward has done, to his credit and to public benefit, is to push us personally to take a hard look at the word "redeem." The root word is "deem," the intellectual challenge to consider, think through and understand deeply. The process of deep intellectual understanding is the challenge of justification and personal truth-seeking. [cogitata perficiendo, cogitando sic perfecta.] The prefix "re" implies repetition, that is, iterations on "deeming." So, "redemption" in its etymological sense means certifying consciousness and coming to personal/ collective justification — what is faith/ reason's common ground.

About justification: I understand "Second Enlightenment" and "Second Coming" in a mutual, co-dependent sense. Christic "Second Coming" is the iteration of Christic First Coming of Jesus; every newborn is a Christ-of-Second-Coming in whom the challenge (passion) of justification (redemption) must be personally "worked through" in the iterations of Second Enlightenment. Redemption and enlightenment collaboratively justify personal, communal living; we may say that the passion of justification is the compassionate process of communal self-realization.

Self-reflection compels us personally to engage the processes of reconciliation/ redemption — faith's ongoing work of holding reason accountable, and reason's ongoing work of holding faith accountable. In the accountability process we come to justified consciousness by which conscience is enlightened and religion redeemed. The "redeemed life" engages the authenticating mechanisms of mutuality, complementarity and subsidiarity, the way beyond the frustration of the Religious Paralysis Syndrome, and the way of living justly.

http://www.gather.com/viewArticle.action?articleId=2814749782 51339

http://www.gather.com/viewArticle.action?articleId=2814749772 89982

To

FELICITAS,

mystical and ever compassionate,

by her students known as

MRS. HAPPY

With God and Nature
Woman ponders the Gospel
Of Earth-Life's Future

Contemplation Modern Style

The more active our lives are, the more we need contemplation. If we fail to take time to contemplate — to think things through — the more likely we are to let tasks run away with us instead of us running tasks.

Global concerns are so many and so consequential. Who can possibly get a handle on them all? At least we must individually do what we can where we are to better things for Mother Nature who sustains all life. Autopoetic Nature, in its here-and-now habit of symbiotic accommodation, deals with the winds of the moment and makes the most of circumstances at hand.

WORD UNLIMITED is not pretentious in intention or expectation. It attempts a realistic approach and outcome, namely, to offer a varied menu of topics that intersect lives of us all at some time or other along the way. The topics are not hodge-podge but neither are they systematized by a rigid, preconceived logic or form. They are rather like an unstructured meditation, open to the Spirit that comes and goes with the winds of the moment.

While the book is structured in Four Sections, Communication, Consciousness, Conscience and Intelligence, the reader might well ask him/ herself at any place how the particular piece is about communication, consciousness, conscience or intelligence, for meditation, no matter in which section, is about the synthesis of Process Rationality.

WORD UNLIMITED modestly presents a body of reflections that might little by little help one root in common ground, and open personal growth into other-consciousness and wellbeing. Let the free Spirit work His/ Her symbiotic way in and with you in your work-a-day life.

I.
COMMUNICATION
GOD IS WORD

The GRACE of Communication is FAITH

II.
CONSCIOUSNESS
GOD is LIGHT

The GRACE of Consciousness is HOPE

III.
CONSCIENCE
GOD is LOVE

The GRACE of Conscience is LOVE

IV.
INTELLIGENCE
GOD is WISDOM

The GRACE of Intelligence is WISDOM

How it is with Trimorphic Resonance

Of one thing be assured, WORD UNLIMITED, God Talk will take you places you've not been before; nevertheless, to places intimately familiar and sensible, for Trimorphic Resonance is the root process of reason, experience and wisdom.

The Sections of the book resonate with each other, as does the subject content of individual topics within Sections. Section Four is about Intelligence, symbiosis and the evolution of wisdom/ theology by way of Trimorphic Resonance. Everything sustainable resonates from within (ab intus) and evolves outwardly from within for all other (pro invicem).

WORD-Communication-FAITH resonates with LIGHT-Consciousness-HOPE, LOVE-Conscience-LOVE; and REASON-Intelligence-WISDOM;

LIGHT-Consciousness-HOPE resonates with LOVE-Conscience-LOVE and WORD-Communication-FAITH; and REASON-Intelligence-WISDOM;

LOVE-Conscience-LOVE resonates with WORD-Communication-FAITH and LIGHT-Consciousness-HOPE, and REASON-Intelligence-WISDOM;

REASON-Intelligence-WISDOM resonates with WORD-Communication-FAITH, and LIGHT-Consciousness-HOPE, LOVE-Conscience-LOVE, for that is the way it is with Ascendant Consciousness in Theological Evolution.

Table of Contents
Free Spirit Reflections

I. FAITH — The Grace of Communication

II. HOPE — the Grace of CONSCIOUSNESS

III. LOVE — the Grace of Conscience

IV. WISDOM — the Grace of Intelligence

AFTERWORD

CONCLUSION

I. FAITH —
The Grace of Communication

DARWIN/ CHARDIN:
A Repeat of the Copernican/Galileoan Debacle

No one questions that Earth is round and not the center of the universe. Roman Catholicism has been unable to digest implications of these truths for centuries and seemingly unable to admit its error even after Pope John Paul II formally and finally apologized for church's sin against Galileo and admitted that evolution is more than theory.

The full sin of the church's avoidance of cosmic evolution still isn't admitted. The Evolutionary Worldview scientifically accepted is the new reality that replaces the Static-Centrist Worldview of medieval theology, and, Darwin and Chardin are the new victims of the church's error. No pope has had the clarity or humility to step forward. No pope publicly mentions the name "Chardin," much less honors his contributions to evolutionary theology. Church's sin against the Jesuit Priest/ Scientist Teilhard de Chardin remains unconfessed. [See Hans Küng, "The Beginning of All Things, Science and Religion," © 2007, Wm B. Eerdmans Publishing Company, Grand Rapids, MI 49505 www.eerdmans.com

Had Hans Küng been elected cardinal instead of his protégé Joseph Ratzinger, the Catholic Church, one might imagine, would be in full admission of its error and would embrace one of its more important scientist/ theologians and the "Theology of Evolution." Hans Küng's book is probably the best and most significant single book on the related matters of the Evolution/ Philosophy/ Theology, to date.

Like no other author, Hans Küng has "analyzed" and "synthesized" the fields of Cosmology/ Philosophy/ Theology as they pertain to evolution. He is historically versed, like few others, in the significant thinkers of all these fields that relate critically to the updating of modern consciousness, precisely what Vatican II called for. ("Gaudium et spes," Intro. #5, § 4.) On the pantheon list of writers of the Eco-Christian Story, Hans Küng deserves top billing.

Cosmic Transformation

It is in the nature of the Cosmos to, always and everywhere, and in all things, send out and receive signals, and thereby to be in perpetual transformation, vertically and horizontally. The sending, receiving, and transforming of signals by way of energy-attenuation is the transformational process of Trimorphic Resonance — the root process revealing Divinity Consciousness.

Signaling, sending and receiving are phenomena of spectrum energy, by which substantiation occurs and transformation happens. The "inside" energetic nature of substance is the means/ end of substance-outsideness, evolving, ever in flux, ever changing. The "outsideness" of substance (body) is qualified in, for and by communication of, with "insideness" (soul.)

It is in the nature of the Cosmos to be inwardly receptive as well as expressive in the perpetual outreach of potential and newness. The Cosmos is all things — energy and outcome perpetually engaged in processing, evolving.

Instinct, Intuition, Intelligence and Accountability

We live in a quantum-electric universe equipped with cortical brains that deal in quantum-electric terms. Instincts are associated with hard-wiring in the ancient avian-reptilian brain, whereas, intuitions are associated with soft-wiring of the cortical brain. Hard-wiring is linear, hot-responsive, which means its reactions to stimuli are direct, immediate, unvarying and uncompromising, as in flight-fight responses and impulsive sex. Soft-wiring in the cortical brain is flexible in response because it is parallel-wired with multiple circuits that draw upon many currents of experience in making decisions. Accountability is a function of intelligence, of intuitional faith/ reason processing, based on best evidence of multi-directional inputs.

The intuitional processing of faith and reason is soft-wired, that is, the outcome of decisions is based on nuanced currents of collective experience. Decisions and outcomes are no less decisive and incisive than reflex hard-wired responses, but, they are better informed to deal with non-linear complexities of immediate circumstances, and less radical, unlike fixed, predictable, iterative responses of instinctive hard-wiring.

The difference between dogmatic fixation in hierarchical, male-absolutist culture and faith/ reason openness is the difference of hard-wired reflex-instinct and soft-wired reflective intuition. Religion is about faith/ reason processing, i.e., engaging the cortical brain, and overriding avian-reptilian instincts. As long as male-absolutist religions impose hard-wired fixations on females and other organic life, rationality and faith will continue to be overreached and violated.

Dominion theology, male-characterized and uncompromising, grounds in reflex iterations of hard-wired instinct, more animal-like than human. Culture and nature are radically bedeviled and compromised by institutional hard-wiring and cannot long be endured. The wheel of culture is forward turning not backward; culturally sanctioned prostitution of nature and women, as in the past, can no longer be abided.

Humankind has the soft-wired circuitry to override the hard-wired irrationality of instincts; it needs to be engaged intentionally. Avian-reptilian brain instincts tend to lock on to dominion-culture, as advanced in the Councils of Trent and Vatican I, whereas, the cortical brain is open to liberation as heralded by the Second Vatican Council. Vatican II advances the mutuality of faith and reason, and the forward-looking currents of open vision; notwithstanding pressures to return to the past, the good sense of Vatican II will have its day.

Religious/ cultural consciousness must adjust even as faith and reason must, as the requirements of love change. Neither faith nor reason compels, much less, justifies fixation in old-world misconceptions that are exposed by new world understandings. I submit that the crises of the times root in dogmatic fixations, in instinctive hard-wiring of static-centrist thinking, i.e., of top-down theology (dominion) and imperial/ feudal culture (compelling submission of the under-privileged to serve the privileged.)

Top-down dominion-theology yet promotes the schism of energy/ matter, soul/ body, and the violent politics of guilt and fear, as advanced in patriarchal history and the exploitation of nature and people. The schism of disconnection, i.e., of spirituality from materiality is destructive and dead-end.

Culturally, humankind and nature together suffer precipitous, mutual self-degradation except nature is respected as the Place of Divine Instance and the Sacrament Condition of humankind and organic life; faith/ reason mutuality accommodates common destinies by way of symbiosis and Eucharistic Purpose engaged in forward thinking, not backward, as in fixation in dogma, cultured absolutism and scriptural literalism.

Redemption and salvation are by way of growth of new life consciousness in the organic humus of misinformed and dying consciousness. Human intuition seeks wholeness beyond the fractured consciousness of instinctive violence. Church is the Global

People seeking wholeness — gentes quaerentes sanitatem. The culture of faith/ reason together in intuitions brought-forward from the past is the Way forward.

Theology Accountable to Faith/ Reason

Change is inherent in the mutual accountability of faith and reason as they continue to test each other. Change of thinking has evolved and continues evolving, but institutions of religion have failed to change commensurate with the advances of faith/ reason. In accepting the advanced changes of faith and reason, the needed changes of institutions should be more obvious. Together, religion and government should facilitate living justified by faith and reason, not frustrated by demands of privilege, alienation and resource exploitation.

Re-envisioning the non-exclusive "Christic Mission" does not demean religious values, or Sacrament, or Eucharist; but the exclusionist presumptions of male-instituted patriarchy do demean them. The change here proposed is to open Judeo-Christian culture from its violent instincts and misinformed perspectives to new insights of faith and reason brought forward intuitively in common.

The original fallacy of Scholastic Theology/ Philosophy underlying cultural violence presumes the male (Adam) as primary (non-corruptible, superior) in the order of the creation-event, and female (Eve) as "secondary," i.e., male-derived and dependent (corruptible, inferior.)

Given evolution's culturally documented pathways to communal wellbeing, the recognition of the essential mutuality of faith (female) and reason (male), each holding the other accountable, should be evident in intuitionally grounded wisdom. Culture based on literalist belief in the Creation/ Fall mythos is clearly misinformed, and (perhaps less clearly) misguided, but misguided, nevertheless.

Argued here is the thesis that the common cause of societal violence, the rape of women and nature through history, roots in the alienation of women (faith) by impassioned, irrational (hard-wired) male reasoning. Belief imposition of the Genesis/ Fall Story claims divine justification contrary to commonsense.

Critically challenged misunderstandings include: creationism vs. evolution; male superiority vs. female inferiority; theology presumed from the top-down vs. organic evolution/ consciousness from the bottom-up; and the revelation of divinity "from within" vs. time-people-selective revelation "from the top-down). Belief in selective divinity revelation is a human artifice. The concept of divinity-consciousness "ab intus" (from within,) includes the unqualified instance and involvement of divinity in the within dynamic of the expanding universe and self-reflective consciousness.

Divine Instance, infinitely and efficiently, graces transformational necessity, including the ascendancy of consciousness beyond natural symbiosis to insights of intentional Eucharistic Altruism. The continuity and mutuality of salvation and redemption is a day-by-day process of fidelity to "the requirements of love," i.e., to the necessity of faith holding reason accountable, and reason holding faith accountable — essential female/ male mutuality.

Sacrament, nature-based and grace-conferring, belongs equally to female/ male persons, and to female/ male characterization distinguishing the "withinness" of every person. The distinction of mutuality extends to individual and personal characterization (complementarity) in the here-and-now circumstances defining potentials and limitations (subsidiarity.)

The hallowed Christian tradition of Trinitarian Godhead-consciousness opens to deeper and more personal understanding by way of Divine Instance operating in the unified realms of physical dynamics (quantum-electric intension) and physical/ psychological dynamics (self-reflective intention), i.e., the ascendancy of

Trimorphic Resonance in the physical/ psychical processing of trustful communication (faith), informed consciousness (hope), and committed conscience (love).

The global dynamic of Trimorphic Resonance can accommodate religions and cultures in their quest of common-ground understandings beyond internecine violence — change we all long for in the deep-heart hopefulness of Godlikeness seeking revelation from within; humankind is nature's interlocutor with divinity and organic life. The trustfulness of organic nature and evolving consciousness gives wings to hope; potentials are aired in trust of nature's intuitional wisdom.

Beyond Hard-wired Patriarchy

If faith and reason grow together in female/ male consciousness, they need to be "concelebrated" in ritual Sacrament as a sign of divine/ human hypostasis. The celebration of Sacrament isn't a "guy" thing, it's about divine/ human covenant; it shouldn't be an ego-event of male one-up-manship over females. Faith is the self-reflective inheritance of intuitional wisdom, intelligently designed in the organic networking and advanced by and sustained in cortical brain processing.

Inclusive Priesthood

Exclusionary clerical celibacy has come on bad times, aggravated by exposures of sexual abuse and cover-up that have been ongoing in male hierarchical culture. The decline in numbers of priests and massive lay attrition are forcing hierarchy and laity alike to question the in-place male-exclusive paradigm of priesthood. The laity increasingly not only sees clericalism as irrelevant but as hurtful to morale and morality. The Church is "The People of God," and the "gates of hell shall not prevail against it." Institutional Roman Catholicism however is less than the whole People under the present paradigm, and there is no guarantee it can survive except it corresponds with the sense of The People (sensus fidelium).

Issues confronting Church now are: can or should the exclusive male priesthood survive; and what changes can and should be made? I answer: male-exclusive, cultic priesthood cannot and should not stand solely; a change of paradigm must occur that is consistent and continuous with the evolving faith/ reason paradigm of divine/ human hypostasis in which the Sacraments of life are "concelebrated" (by males and females together) in continuity with the intuitional faith/ reason of females and males.

On the issue of relevance and irrelevance: to be relevant means to be competent and informed in servicing the needs of the people. It is reasonable to observe that priesthood is relevant to the extent that it meets the needs of the people in the contexts of time and place, and it is irrelevant to the extent that it loses context in time and place and fails the needs of the people.

Roman Catholicism's cultic priesthood has lost sense of time/ place context because of its theological elaboration grounded in presumed male-superior ontology, and primacy place in the divine/ human relationship. Theological elaborations based on the more than 2000 year-old worldview have lost relevance in context of today's worldview consciousness. Priesthood is in crisis because of its failure of mission, that is, to make relevant to the people their relatedness to one another in the organic context of the Naturalis Sacramentum Ordinis.

The failure of cultic priesthood is manifest in its complicit justification of the exploitation of nature by self-interest profiteering, i.e., feudal, colonial, and corporate capitalism, and the exclusion of women from equivalent standing with males. In the Sacrament of Natural Order it is absurd to deny and derogate the essential ontology of female/ male agency in the origin and maintenance of sustainable life. No aspect of organic life is male-exclusive, except in the hard-wired artifice of theological presumption.

Nature is the sustainable means of all life and the grace-conferring condition of human consciousness. Humankind belongs to nature, comes from nature and returns to nature. The demeaning of nature in any regard demeans the human person. The demeaning of females by self-elective presumptions of male-priesthood radically alienates females from their rightful place of Eucharistic service and undermines the fabric of social/ cultural bonding.

The male order of cultic priesthood is rightly questioned at the present time. Cultic priesthood is counter-intuitive and should not continue because it is based on a schismatic, fictional paradigm of male super-arrogation. If male-exclusive priesthood is based on a fictional paradigm, is there an authentic (non-fictional) paradigm that can replace it? A new, replacement-paradigm, consistent with essential female/ male co-dependency/ equivalency, is presently and universally accessible.

Faith/ Reason: neither, superior nor inferior

The Creation/ Fall Mythos in the Book of Genesis speaks to the ongoing need for redemption and salvation; in that regard, every community, every person regardless of age or sex, is an agent (subject) and agendum (object), both, enabling community and enabled by community.

In community, every person is of equal personality by birth, in need, and in grace. It is therefore right and proper for female persons, in equal standing with males, to witness in "con-celebration" the memorial events of life (Sacraments) common to all from birth to death. Life's universal dynamics of nature and nurture implicate everyone in common ways and by common means; and everyone, as agent and agendum in vital processing, needs to receive and give uplift to one another.

By the harmonized witness of female/ male con-celebration of Sacraments, all are reminded that each is grace to other, and each is repository of spiritual gifts received from ancestors to be passed on individually from one generation to the next. In the communal celebration of two-someness, of female/ male together, faith/ reason together, con-celebrating Sacrament in community, is represented Trinitarian Godhead in human family/ community. Priesthood and parenthood together, as Sacrament of nature/ nurture, re-present and are the spiritual/ material reality of Eucharist in Process — divine/ human hypostasis uplifting life and consciousness.

Toward a New Paradigm: CON-CELEBRATING Sacrament

The evolution of organic life involves the continuity processes of complexity and the enlargement of human potential by way spiritual/ material differentiation. The evolution of genetic complexity in the process of reproduction enables the expansion of opportunistic transformation within interdependent limits of organic life, above the (hard-wired) reflexes of physical/ chemical intensionality to the open-ended intentionality of self-reflective, sensible community.

The sense and sensibility of self-reflective humanity, female/male, constitute the ground of religion and the con-celebratory capacity of the female/male characterized person. Paradigmatic Nature, in all matters physical and spiritual, grounds in the reality of the two sexes and the personal disposition of all persons as female/ male-characterized. Intuitional self-reflectivity is processed equivalently in the brains of females and males.

In woman and man, the human brain continuously deals with matters, sacred and profane, none of which is exclusive to woman or man, but which are authentically disposed by mutual fidelity to common interests of personal/ social wellbeing and sustainability. The con-celebration of sacred remembrances (Sacraments) is equally compelling for females and males, together committed to lives of service to each other and community, and to sustaining resources of other life in the organic interactions of web ecologies commonly essential to all life. The discerning of wellbeing and of making morally justified decisions/ choices involves the faith/reason processes of communication, consciousness and conscience.

Religious (moral) relationships that qualify the mutuality and complementarity of both sexes is a paradigm that envisions an inclusive priesthood that is more representative of the dynamics of female/ male mutuality/ complementarity; female/ male con-celebration of matters spiritual and physical better reflects the harmony of Godlike community.

Ritual Sacraments are common participatory events that call for con-celebration. "Sacraments of Nature" (baptism, anointing, Eucharist) define the conferring graces of Eucharistic Sacrament from birth (baptism) to death (anointing). Eucharist is the over-arching Sacrament of Nature.

"Sacraments of Nurture," reconciliation-confession, commitment-confirmation, and marriage-priesthood-covenant, are about communal dynamics of mutual interactions, and communal authentication by way of the celebratory uplift of mutuality and complementarity. The Sacraments of Nurture impose equally on all the urgency to attain maturity and sense of social/ personal duty in fidelity to ongoing reconciliation, commitment and trust-obligations to family, community and nature. Priesthood, like the husband/ wife trust commitment, celebrates the bonded twoness of woman/ man in the sacred process of producing and providing for soul/ body needs of newborns and everyone from birth to death — what is the Eucharistic Altruism of "Second Comings."

IF WE BELIEVE IN A PERSONAL FUTURE

we would refuse to be imprisoned in the past. If we believe religion has a future we would focus on the future. Instead, we focus on the past and are stopped in our tracks.

And wherein is the destiny of the future? It is in children of today. Religion that fails the children of today destines itself to failure. A major problem of religion is that it fails by self-imprisonment in the past. Postmodernity is projecting into the future at such a rapid pace (and its children with it) that institutional religion focused in the past is fast becoming irrelevant.

Mental deadness from habituated fixation in the past is an occupational disease more of males than of females. Giving birth to new life and nurturing new life is the perpetual concern of females; celibate male culture, intentionally self-disconnected from the future, is a deadening load on church, culture and the future.

All women, especially Religious Orders of women, true to their feminine nature, are deeply sensitive to children and family. Theirs is the naturally-directed future focus, and the organizing presence of previsioning human necessities. Woman's femininity is symbiotically harmonious with ecozoic femininity. Nature is being mortally wasted by corporate commercial exploitation, facilitated by complicity of religious culture backward fixated in the alienation of women and a benighted attitude toward nature.

Women religious are the hope of the future for they have the natural instincts and intuitions of essential human connectedness to nature. True religion is expressed in faithfully securing Earth necessities upon which all futurity relies.

Culturally, we entangle ourselves in backward preoccupation and consume Earth and each other as if there were no tomorrow, and we remain prisoners of the past.

Doing Theology, Extra-institutionally

Until now the "hermeneutic of continuity" has been applied from first beginnings of doing theology in the Roman Catholic Tradition. The continuous development of theology from first beginnings until now presumes absolute and unchanging truth with foundations in the Genesis account of the Creation of the cosmos, life, Eve from Adam and first sin of Eve and Adam. As new theology was developed through the centuries, it always tied back to first theology. First theology understands inadequately how the Tree of Life greens faithfully, consistently, generation after generation.

Faith and theological truth are presumed to be continuous from first revelations in Old Testament history, also as pertains to the understanding of God/ creation/ humanity. Evolution is nowhere accommodated in first understandings, nor in the hermeneutics of theological continuity. Ancient science could not possibly own understandings that are commonplace today. There are fixed conceptual understandings already in first theology that are handed down in the continuity process by hierarchical theologians who build new theology on premises and presumptions of the old. Clearly, the worldview that is presumed in traditional Catholic Theology is unaccommodating to the theological consciousness of the evolutionary worldview.

Today, no serious theologian accepts literally the myths of Genesis that embody the theological presumptions brought forward in Catholic Tradition. The radical presumptions of Old Testament/ New Testament science root in the worldview of the time, which makes no sense to modern evolutionary science.

The theologians of today, male and female, are constrained to do theology intra-institutionally, i.e., keeping within the presumptive process of linking all new theology back to prior theological assumptions for purposes of preserving the continuity of the first theological hermeneutic. Thus, the worldview of Aristotle/ Aquinas is still the presumptive and required basis of Roman Catholic Theology.

The conundrum is that church has tied itself in knots of its own making by closing the door from the beginning to any future possibility of worldview change. The very word "evolution" has been anathema since Vatican I; and doing theology outside the presumptions of the static-centrist worldview (Scholastic Philosophy) is "anathema" because it is "outside" the "hermeneutic of continuity." Any theologian who attempts to do a theology of theistic evolution is "anathema" because (s)he is doing theology that is outside institutional hermeneutics, i.e., extra-institutional.

The tradition of closed Catholic Theology is a product of all-male (incestuous) thinking that imposes on God the idolatry of conformity to male prerogation. This writer recognizes that no theologian has institutional coinage if (s)he does extra-institutional theology — and theistic evolution does extra-institutional theology; notwithstanding this understanding, and even though I claim no theological professionalism, I have made it my lifework to accommodate evolution science to the teachings of Jesus, the Christ. Until now my endeavors enjoy little regard even though the truths of evolution science accommodate open theology better than the archaic and mistaken presumptions of Scholastic Philosophy.

www.divinicom.com; www.secondenlightenment.org; www.evolution101.org

Failed Civility, Failed Religion

Incivility, like a fever, is a sure sign of diseased religion. Civility is a sign of authentic relationship; incivility is a sign of inauthentic relationship, failed religion. The diseased condition of global society, of global ecology, is a sure sign of religious inauthenticity, religious failure. Civil society isn't possible except for citizens seeking to be religiously authentic in their relationships with each other and nature.

Religion is about moral imagination, what it means to be "Godlike." The Trinitarian Thesis of faith/hope/love in Godhead likeness is frustrated by ungodly ignorance, arrogance and obsession. Godlikeness is pursued in the intentional processing of trustful communication, informed consciousness, and committed conscience. Ignorance is antithetical to trustful communication, arrogance is antithetical to informed consciousness, and obsession is antithetical to committed conscience. Where culture is infected with ignorance, arrogance and obsession, irreligion and incivility prevail. Fixation in ignorance, arrogance and obsession is a blight of the dominion culture, of Abrahamic inheritance.

Patriarchal culture and dominion theology enable religious inauthenticity and civil violence by imposing on people the requirement of obedience to doctrinaire theology and patriarchal presumption. The first doctrine of patriarchy is the divine election of males and the subordination of females. The theology of dominion does not give females equivalent recognition in the religious/ cultural processing of communication (faith), consciousness (hope), and conscience (love.) Judaism, Christianity and Islam dominate unjustly against the equal participation of women in religion (theology) and politics (ecclesiology.)

The religious/ cultural alienation of women is equally frustrating to religion as it is to civility. The remedy is to acknowledge the mutuality of faith (femininity) and reason (masculinity) in the harmonious pursuit of religion and civility. In effect, what this implies is that the processing of faith and reason is continuous AND EVOLVING. The setting of the mind against evolution is fixation in ignorance, arrogance and obsession. The culture of fixation is the culture of Antithetical Trinity and the frustration of the Trinitarian Thesis.

Evolution is the condition of faith/reason mutuality, of civil/religious mutuality, of female/male authenticity.

http://www.gather.com/viewArticle.action?articleId=2814749794 04112

Faith/Reason Conflict

Distrust, like schizophrenia, is a disease of conflicted consciousness, of the adversary relationship between faith and reason. Patriarchal culture behaves distrustfully toward women. The contradictory signals of faith and reason are personally and culturally unsettling, and are unremitting sources of frustration. Cultured distrust and alienation instill angst and anger, and they work out their psychological damage in frustrations of interpersonal and familial relationships.

The unrelenting word wars between faith and reason are waged in the venue of personal conscience and public consciousness — between authoritarianism and the personal struggle for self-authentication. The unforgiving expectations of patriarchal over-lording violently insult personal conscience and consciousness. The suppressive voice of patriarchal repression insults and aggravates proclivities toward depression. The persistent aggression of insult hits on defenses of natural immunities and weakens them against psychological damage.

The first step to healing psychological injury is escape from an environment of hostility, aggression and suppression to a friendly and hopeful environment conducive to good faith and reason. Hope is a precondition to the healing of depression and the restoration of normal relationship between faith and reason — and hope isn't enabled EXCEPT FOR TRUST. Before healing, hope must prevail; before hope can prevail trust must mediate faith and reason, hurt and healing, the parent/ child relationship — the authoritarian/ dependent relationship.

Hope is the medicine of recovery. Hope enlightens the future with possibilities. The frustration of hope is a consignment to endless suppression, repression and depression — the perpetual exposure to aggravated insult and the breakdown of defenses that depend on the functional harmony of faith and reason.

Trust is the two-way street of mutuality. When expectations are channeled down a one-way street, conflict and loss of self-reliance result. Authoritarian fideism is a one-way street of suppression, repression and depression, the aggravation of schizophrenia and the frustration of selfhood. On the face of it, schizophrenia is the aggravated disease of animus between faith and reason. Churches! Stop aggravating the disease of schizophrenia on your global people! Open the avenues of trust to female/ male mutuality!

Faith is Freedom from Fear

Arguably the single-most empowering aspect of faith is its grace to overcome fear. The disabling power of fear is faith's greatest frustration. The theology and culture of dominion derives from patriarchal awareness of fear as an effective device to disempower people and bring them under physical/mental submission. The way of keeping fear at a fever pitch is to exact rules and faith expectations that keep people on edge for the fear of consequences from non-compliance.

Old Testament Scripture is a history of patriarchy's cult of guilt and fear. The detail and numbers of ancient requirements impose on the people even now. Under the Roman Empire, as with empires of all time, laws and regulations were imposed and enforced by threats of torture and mortal punishment. Especially cruel and violent were torture and death by crucifixion. The Jewish people especially were victimized. Incredibly, the imperial culture of Roman Catholicism chose to use control devices of guilt and fear by imposing faith-expectations and behavior requirements, including extreme means of inquisition, mental torture and excommunication. This unchristian practice is not reconcilable with the teaching and example of the crucified Jesus.

This final violent vestige of imperial religious culture is totally antithetical to what Christianity means and is. All Christians of good faith should revolt against the sin of violent authoritarianism that flies in the face of Jesus's example and teaching to love one another and support each other in truth and justice.

Of all religions, Christians should be first to reject the anti-Christian devices of guilt and fear, and should witness tolerance and acceptance of other. Called for are compassion, acceptance and thankfulness for the heroic witness of others to the primacy of personal conscience. Christian churches are not Christian when they use guilt and fear to violate the personal consciences of others.

http://ncronline.org/news/women/maryknoll-gives-bourgeois-notice-removal-order

http://www.gather.com/viewArticle.action?articleId=2814749793 52523

The Accountable Theology of Faith/ Reason

An objection to GREEN RELIGION and the Evolution Trilogies is raised that they mean to change everything; yes, to the extent that evolved concepts open to new and authentic Christian understandings.

http://www.gather.com/viewArticle.action?articleId=2814749792 28518

I will set forth and specify "conceptual" changes I mean. Change is inherent in the mutual accountability of faith and reason as they continue to test each other. Change of thinking has evolved and continues evolving but institutions have not changed commensurate to the mutual advances of faith/ reason. In opening up to advances of faith and reason, needed institutional changes should be more obvious. Together, religion and culture should facilitate living justified by faith and reason, not frustrate them by demands of privilege, alienation and resource exploitation.

Envisioning a universal "Christic mission" does not demean religious valuation or Sacrament and Eucharist, but, exclusionist presumptions of male-instituted patriarchy do demean religious consciousness. The change I propose is to open Judeo-Christian culture from misinformed perspectives and instincts of violence to new insights of compassion and mutuality. The original fallacy of Scholastic Theology/ Philosophy underlying cultural misdirection is the Original alienation of man/ woman.

Given historically documented pathways to communal wellbeing, the recognition of the essential mutuality of faith (female) and reason (male), each holding the other accountable, should be evident in intuitionally grounded wisdom. Culture based on literalist belief in the Creation/ Fall mythos is clearly misinformed, and (perhaps less clearly) misguided, but misguided, nevertheless. Argued here is the thesis that the common cause of societal violence, the rape of women and nature through history, root in the cultured alienation of women by impassioned irrational males. This tragic fixation in myth claims divine justification in the Genesis Creation/ Fall Story.

Dualistic misunderstandings include: creationism vs. evolution; male priority vs. female inferiority; top-down theology vs. bottom-up organic evolution/ consciousness; and divinity revelation "from within" vs. time-people-elective revelation. The notion of arbitrary divinity is a human fiction. The concept of divinity-consciousness "ab intus", from within, includes the instance and involvement of divinity in the within dynamic of the expanding universe and consciousness.

Divine Instance, infinitely and efficiently graces transformational necessity, including the ascendancy of consciousness beyond natural symbiosis to the insight of intentional Eucharistic Altruism. The continuity and mutuality of salvation and redemption are day-by-day processes responsive to love's requirements, i.e., to the necessity of faith holding reason accountable, and reason holding faith accountable — what is the essential meaning of female/ male mutuality.

Sacrament, nature-based and grace-conferring, belongs equally to female/ male persons, and to female/ male characterization distinguishing the "withinness" of every person. The distinction of mutuality extends to individual and personal characterization (complementarity) in the here-and-now circumstances defining potentials and limitations (subsidiarity.)

The hallowed Christian tradition of Trinitarian Godhead-consciousness opens to deeper and more personal understanding by way of Divine Instance operating in the unified realms of physical dynamics (quantum-electric intension) and physiological/ psychological dynamics (self-reflective intention), i.e., the ascendancy of Trimorphic Resonance in the physical/ psychical processing of trustful communication (faith), informed consciousness (hope), and committed conscience (love).

The global dynamic of Trimorphic Resonance can accommodate religions and cultures in their common-ground understandings beyond lethal internecine violence — change we all long for in the deep-heart hopefulness of Godlikeness seeking revelation from within; humankind is nature's interlocutor with divinity and organic life. The trustfulness of organic nature and evolving consciousness gives wings to hope and air to discovering and trusting deep nature's intuitions.

EUCHARIST: Getting inside Each Other

Social relationships are about "getting inside each other." We are all cocooned within a network of people and diverse life — which provides daily exchange and change, whether in actions doing things together, or exchanging ideas, hopes, fears, etc. We can't help but get inside each other.

The way we get inside each other profoundly affects whether peace or conflict occupies our soul, our consciousness. What we say and do influences the soul of others and what they do and are. It is true that we become the person of the company we keep, of the environment we live in.

Whether we realize it or not, symbiosis constantly impacts every life, for better or for worse. By our sensitivity for and to others, the character of symbiotic living is determined; this expands out into the larger world in terms of how we see, understand and use or abuse the symbiotic webs of diverse life that link all globally. Embedded in specifically diverse webs of the region, we are a force that brings about change. The Sacrament of Intentional Eucharist is about personal commitment to be agents of change for the better, not for the worse.

TALK: About Honesty, Healing

Trustful communication, especially the trustfulness of confessional conversation is a powerful balm of healing. Communication is always about information-exchange, a way of expanding on learning and of maintaining stable relations.

The family setting is the place where the most meaningful conversations take place — in how to uplift one another and bring healing to self and other. For reasons of personal dispositions, incomplete knowledge and misinformation, we all have rough edges that grate on others. Civility, religion and family harmony call for honest exchanges that mitigate hurts, whether from intentional or inadvertent conversations.

Conversations that heal should be the hallmark of communication between parents and children, for children become the personalities of their parents in mannerisms of speech, thought and behavior.

It is well that families set aside times, weekly, daily, as needed, to talk through hurts one or another is holding inside due to events and words exchanged. Little unhealed hurts become big hurts if the medicine of love isn't early and regularly applied. Interpersonal confession is a continuous and necessary part of healing hearts and mind. Apologies are always in order as circumstances require.

TALK: About Promise, Commitment

If we develop an eye for seeing unfinished work, whether chores, projects or strained relationships, we do well to deal with them before moving on to other things. Nature is the BIG unfinished work project.

Religion, family and community work for the same reasons, namely, for reasons of mature commitment that we bring to interpersonal relationships, including and especially about those things we all depend on in common, in matters of the health of diverse webs of life and the environment. Living nature is not only a practical resource for bodily needs, but also provides inspiration and pleasure, for the beauty, song and diversion in it. Gardens are not just to produce food but are places of soul-nourishment and wonder — access to mystery and mysticism as we dig more deeply into life's intricacies in soil and symbiotic organisms.

We need the surprise, the playfulness of nature; we owe promise to nature as much as nature owes promise to us — the same is true about the promise we owe each other — commitment, promise, is what the Sacrament of Confirmation is about.

IDENTITY

Identity begins with self-discovery and recognition of place in the Sacrament of Natural Order. In God's Image every individual person is characterized female/ male, whether of male or a female gender. Until we get Godhead consciousness right and our place in nature right, we get religion wrong.

All other discussions aside, until human self-discovery recognizes that every individual is female/ male characterized, we deceive ourselves. Contrary to Thomistic Theology, between male and female, relationship is neither primary nor secondary, but equal. Church ignorance to the contrary is culpable and inexcusable. Evolution is a reality. www.divinicom.com

Until the matter of self-identity is cleared up and recognized by church hierarchy, the theology and ecclesiology of church will continue to divide, alienate, and be at odds with the personal self internally.

The Nature of Grace

If the dictum is accepted that "grace supposes nature", then it must be recognized that one's personal relationship with nature is an essential component of mature religious commitment, Confirmation. Ignorance of nature clouds the consciousness of grace and the role one can and should play in the grace-nature relationship. An authentic sense of place is frustrated if one is clueless about the Sacrament of Natural Order. Medieval theology is cleaved with misinformed dualities that deceive.

The grace of Sacrament presumes an understanding of rightly ordered relationship. The purpose and content of Confirmation needs urgently to be reconsidered in light of the fundamental truth that grace of Sacrament supposes grace of nature. Age and maturity coincide with a capacity to grasp the essential correlation of grace as sacred and natural. A lifetime focused on fidelity to this correlation is a commitment proper to Confirmation.

PSYCHIC EVOLUTION: The Dynamic Soul of Green Religion

The self-affirmation of personal authenticity is by way of entering into the spectrum energy of "green religion," the vitality in-common of organic life. What is "green religion?" Green religion is about organic (self-reflective) consciousness of interdependent relationships. Reality is relationship; religion is about the mindfulness of common relationships, about functional harmony. In the context of universal resourcing, the psychic energy of self-reflection can bring one to the intentional and fulfilling insight of Eucharistic Altruism.

By meditating a few minutes a day, the first thing in the morning, specifically, on the "insidedness" of spectrum energy," one can discover new vision and new energy in daily living.

The book "GREEN RELIGION, Inside the Cultural Spectrum," is arranged in short readings for each day of the week, over a period of 21 weeks. Bite-size reflection in this way gives one enough to "chew on" for the day, without too much at a time. One can edge into a deeper sense of belonging to self, to other, and to nature, without feeling dread and heaviness. To be "at home" in the cultural spectrum is to flow with nature's resonant power of electromagnetism and be vitalized by it.

There is so much to be gained by doing a brief daily meditation, and so much to be missed by not doing it. This is a grassroots way of entering real life, down-to-earth theology, "from the bottom up." It is the natural way of enlightenment and the authentication of self and other.

Sylvester L Steffen

http://www.authorhouse.com/Bookstore/BookDetail.
aspx?Book=291520

America's Crisis

America's crisis, the global economic crisis is primarily a crisis of ecology, of failed personal/ collective conscience in the use of natural resources. Unless we personally discover hands-on relationships with nature/ ecology, there's little chance we can dispel the culture of ignorance and arrogance rooted in the cultural experience of unbridled corporate capitalism.

We need to return our souls and our hands to earth-connection. Specifically, we need to understand agriculture as something we all can do and all need to do — for our own and for nature's health. If we but look, there are more resource opportunities at hand than we realize. The accumulated goodness of little acts to help nature, stressed species, become big acts. Agriculture at all levels needs human energy and less fossil fuel energy. God spare us if we continue the status-quo road to ecological, political, religious and cultural waste and destruction. It starts with change of soul, with personal religious conversion/ redemption.

http://www.gather.com/viewArticle.action?articleId=281474978
251339

Asking the Unaskable

One gets a sense that irreligious arrogance (malice) is behind Earth's cancer of out-of-control human population. Tell me, do some religions explicitly promote prolix reproduction for the purpose of becoming "religiously" dominant? I put the question directly to Roman Catholicism and Islam. If they do, they should stop it, for God's sake! Such arrogance (malice) is despicable for it ultimately leads to violence, self-destruction and the destruction of global life. The virtue of moderation compels moral sensitivity in avoiding overreach that suffocates the ecological bases of Earth-life as it has come to flourish. Religions! Get your act together. Realize, imperious male bachelorhood is a plague on faith and reason. Male self-arrogation on presumption of Biblical absolutism is neither reasonable nor sustainable.

What is "Sustainable?"

The word sustainable in the ecological context has to take into consideration "sustainable populations" as populations relate to each other in complex web-interrelationships. The most destructive and unsustainable thing about Planet Earth at this time is the absolute domination of excess human populations and the mindless waste of species and ecologies. Coupled with corporate capitalism, the mindlessness of out-of-control human populations is putting life on Planet Earth on a collapse course.

Moral conversation about sustainability is meaningless if humankind side-steps the destructive momentum of ignorance and denial, and takes this elephant-in-the-room off the table of discussion.

http://ncronline.org/blogs/eco-catholic/what-does-%E2%80%98sustainability%E2%80%99-mean

http://onpoint.wbur.org/2011/04/26/pentagon-security

"It is time for America to re-focus our national interests and principles through a long lens on the global environment of tomorrow. It is time to move beyond a strategy of containment to a strategy of sustainment (sustainability); from an emphasis on power and control to an emphasis on strength and influence; from a defensive posture of exclusion, to a proactive posture of engagement. We must recognize that security means more than defense, and sustaining security requires adaptation and evolution (emphasis added), the leverage of converging interests and interdependencies. To grow we must accept that competitors are not necessarily adversaries, and that a winner does not demand a loser. We must regain our credibility as a leader among peers, a beacon of hope, rather than an island fortress. It is only by balancing our interests with our principles that we can truly hope to sustain our growth as a nation and to restore our credibility as a world leader."

"...we need to focus on sustaining ourselves in ways that build our strengths and underpin credible influence. That shift in turn means that the starting point for our strategy should be internal rather than external. The 2010 National Security Strategy did indeed focus on national renewal and global leadership, but this account makes an even stronger case for why we have to focus first and foremost on investing our resources domestically in those national resources that can be sustained, such as our youth and our natural resources (ranging from crops, livestock, and potable water to sources of energy and materials for industry). We can and must still engage internationally, of course, but only after a careful weighing of costs and benefits and with as many partners as possible. Credible influence also requires that we model the behavior we recommend for others, and that we pay close attention to the gap between our words and our deeds."

Divinity/ Motherhood: the Mystery of ISNESS

I write this on Mother's Day, May 8, 2011. What is the relationship of Divinity to all existence? [By Divinity I mean God.] We learn about Divinity from the experience of life, from the process of life ever in forward (time/ space) movement. There are three aspects of evolving nature that are telling about Divinity Virtue; these are: INsistence, PERsistence and CONsistence. [See GREEN RELIGION, pg. 205]

INSISTENCE: Divine Presence is sensed in Insistence, the "withinness" of cosmic dynamics. The universe is expanding at the speed of light, outwardly and from within; the division of cells and organic growth are from within. Universal expansion and organic growth "from within," speak to the in-sistence of Divine Instance, the existential priority of the universe. The movement of in-sistence is future-directed not in fixation of status-quo conformity; insistence in status-quo fixation is nonsensical on its face.

PERSISTENCE: That which was "before" perdures in that which is "after;" as Einstein says, "$E=MC^2$", which states the identity and relationship of all "isness" in common origin; all that was before, and is after, is energy in process of substantive transformation. Matter is the perpetually changing derivative of energy and is complexly defined even as energy is refined in its qualification. "Ensoulment" is energy qualified as the "withinness" of all substance, by which allness communally endures.

CONSISTENCE: The outcome of insistent persistence is consistence. Consistency does not mean sameness, uniformity and conformity of relationships, for the dynamics of relationships seek openness and divergence as well as convergence and emergence. Convergence, divergence and emergence expand the complexity nature of qualified energy in consciousness, and advances self-reflectivity. The direction of self-reflectivity is "ascendant", that is, toward discerning cause-and-effect relationships and the "purposefulness" of relationships; self-reflectivity is, at its basic sense, a reflection of Divinity Consciousness.

The perfecting of Divinity Consciousness is a transformational process of moral imagination, of discernment that invites "Godlikeness" by way of resonant accommodation, i.e., the "Trimorphic Resonance" of communication (faith), consciousness (hope) and conscience (love). The single word that best defines the holistic process of purposeful evolution and becoming more Godlike, is "EUCHARIST."

All exists for all; all exists in all; all reflectivity is the conscious insideness of evolving energy/ matter. The ascendancy of consciousness is by way of unity (INsistence), community (PERsistence), and continuity (CONsistence). Humanity progresses in ascendant consciousness when faith holds reason accountable, and when reason holds faith accountable.

Irrationality happens when faith gives reason free license; fideism happens when reason gives faith free license. Fideism and irrationality are trademarks of "dominionism", the culture of patriarchal empire that alienates faith and reason, women and men, and universally bedevils nature and humanity. Except for accountability to the "Divinely Maternal" — males accountable to females, females accountable to males, and both accountable to nature — life is frustrated in Divinity Consciousness growth; except for Divinity Consciousness, "religion" is meaningless. Motherhood virtues are INsistence, PERsistence, and CONsi-stence. www.divinicom.com

Is Sacrament Reality or Theatre?

Sacrament is betrayed when ritual is confused for reality. The pomp and circumstance of ritual is no substitute for natural reality. This truth needs to be grasped if the way forward would be illumined.

In general, we arrive on Earth one at a time and leave one at a time, no pomp, no circumstance. Population numbers are affected by how long people hang around between coming and going. Now that we old codgers live a lot longer and the global population of the young is swelling, the pressure on global economies and ecologies is really problematic; politicians and people of faith are getting unsettled. The middle-age population group is fearful of the tsunami at the opposite ends of the age spectrum. The big splash is coming, and neither religion nor politics have a handle. The reality of the dilemma is ecological and moral, and moral imagination alone doesn't resolve the way forward; "faith" in its traditional casting is ill-equipped to find the moral way, and politics-as-usual bungles.

Believers (politics) today are no different now than in the past. Because religious belief is institutionally defined and controlled more in institutional-interest, it looks backward more than forward. People have been satisfied to let institutions have their way; their faith is fideism, a kind of fatalistic resignation accepting that institutions know best, so we go along with them. Like church institutions, people are in denial of their complicit sin of wasting nature and bringing Earth-life to the brink of unrecoverable destruction.

Neither the moralizing of the Religious Right nor the theological politics of "increase-and-multiply" are up to dealing with the crisis; the moral imagination of both fails to anticipate the consequences of complacent complicity. The hubris of the Garden Mandate "increase and multiply" blinds conscience from seeing the equally urgent mandate "not to consume the fruit of the middle tree" (web-life ecology) and destroy it; reality needs and expects faith and commonsense, not the wishful piety of fideism.

The fideism of cultic hubris (male-hierarchy) is not only irrational, anti-social and radically insane (unhealthy), but it is also intoxicatingly numbing in its capacity to disengage moral imagination and keep people in the twilight zone. Where are the churches? They are peddling the unhealthy diet of preoccupation with sex, money and mind control. As in times past, the placebo of mind-control diseases the soul with sugar diabetes, even as it disarms moral righteousness from taking a stand against faux faith.

Maybe the tide of public consciousness is shifting. Maybe the people are coming to their moral senses and beginning to recognize their predicament and its causes. There is no grace in the surfeit of numbers, but there is grace in the religious commitment to preserve the sustaining means of life on Earth.

The new moral imagination needed is consciousness of Eucharistic

Altruism. Sacrament is reality, not theatre. Spiritual obesity is theatrical leisure that valuates ritual enactment above reality. True Sacrament is true reality, and the reality is that population numbers are out of control, and global nature is at risk of being ultimately wasted. People! What are we going to do about it? Leaving it to churches and politicians is no answer. It's time we all try to be more Godlike in thinking and doing, in personal living. www.divinicom. com

The Ordination Controversy in the Roman Catholic Church

As the all-male hierarchy of the Roman Catholic Church is construed, the official position is that the male hierarchy is without authority to ordain women. This is the stated, unambiguous position of Popes John Paul II and Benedict XVI. They have closed this position to further discussion. So, what option is left for women to claim equal authenticity with males in the servant-priesthood of the Catholic Church? The faithful believe that "the gates of hell shall not prevail" against The Church, understood as God's People committed to "love one another" as Jesus loved and served the whole people.

The Roman Catholic male hierarchy has staked its claim of exclusionary right but with acknowledgement of no authority in women's claim of inclusionary right in the priesthood of The Church, the People Church of Catholic Eucharist. In the context of Imperial Rome, the Jesus-People-Church was subsumed under the imperial culture of Rome, the very Empire that crucified Jesus.

This writer has taken the position that women, on their own authority, should define their inclusionary position in the servant-priesthood of the Eucharistic Catholic Church, and, formulate an appropriate ritual of ordination that anoints their inclusionary right and responsibility in the Sacrament of Natural Order. It is puzzling that women would want to be ordained under the male-exclusionary ritual of Roman

Catholicism as presently construed, and that males are blind to the alienation and hurt the people suffer from exclusionism.

Women, as "Mothers of Heralds of the Gospel" are commissioned to teach the Jesus-Gospel to their sons and daughters, both in regard to the non-exclusionary teaching of Jesus and as to the alienating culture of male imperial priesthood. The controversy, by this approach, may in time be resolved through the working of the Holy Spirit in the minds and hearts of future generations of "Heralds of the Gospel," and their mothers.

The ordination controversy is corrosive and so unnecessary. On this controversy my position is clear: as the Roman Catholic Church-priesthood is construed, I do not advocate for women's ordination. Notwithstanding this position, it is my belief, that "in the person" of Mary, Mother of the WORD, women are the primary "Heralds of the Gospel," primary servant-priests.

It might be expected that coming generations of young men and women may chose not to be part of the exclusionary priesthood. Fair-minded people are likely to conclude that women have just cause to take issue with the male hierarchy as presently construed in Roman Catholicism, in conflict with the Eucharistic Gospel of Jesus, the Cosmic Christ.

The Real Message

There is no likelihood that the hierarchy will change in the foreseeable future its culture of cover-up which has enabled it to deceive people in matters profane and religious. Instantaneous global person-to-person communication may drive institutions of religion to transparency as they experience radical implosion. But who can wait? And, why wait?

Not to despair; Eucharist is more than words. Jesus commissions us personally to be Eucharist to each other. It is action that matters;

words alone are ineffectual. We are all ordained to the priesthood of action.

FANNING FLAMES of ENDTIME FEARS

In times of desperation, politics and religion find convergence. Right wing politics in our time curries favor with right wing religion. In this election cycle they are tending toward the religion/ politics of fear and apocalyptic obsession; together they monger end-time fears, Apocalypse now.

As the saying goes, about three things we can be certain, life, death and taxes. Life supposes nature as nature supposes death. Except for death, there is no evolution and renewal of life, no Resurrection. With death and rebirth come the ascendancy of consciousness and its associated graces, faith, hope and love.

The mutual indebtedness of all to life and death is a sign of common obligation, of common indenture without absolute claim to anything material: "dust thou art, and to dust thou shalt return."

The pearl of great price is Spirit, Ascendant Consciousness, which enables dust to breathe and be WORD-Made-Flesh. The common tax imposed on self-reflective life for the privilege of Ascendant Consciousness is return of Earth substance to perpetual rebirth.

Ego-obsession in the stuff-of-life is the arrogance of ignorance, a problem of religion and politics. The political "Religious Right" is the "religious wrong" because it is ego-obsessed. Its target now is President Obama, and by association Oprah Winfrey and what is not "white;" the implication that white is "religiously right." The antithesis to divinity is self-possessed ego-centrism, the satanic anti-trinity of ignorance, arrogance and obsession.

II. HOPE —
the Grace of CONSCIOUSNESS

Non-Denominational Sacrament/ Eucharist

Institutions do not own theology, people do. Institutions do not "do" theology, people do. Consciousness of cosmic reality reveals the inner urgency of evolution, its purpose and the meaning of Eucharist. Remembrance and purpose are complicit in self-reflective consciousness, in Sacrament. Static consciousness deactivates self-reflectivity. The deactivation of self-reflection stultifies; at this time the Vatican seeks fixity in the theology of the Councils of Trent and the First Vatican. The Vatican can neither hold up nor appropriate the natural processes of the Sacrament of Evolution.

"Theistic evolution" is an evolved insight acquired from the experience of evolutionary purpose and outcomes of intentional actions taken. Self-reflectivity remembers experiences of inner compulsion toward moral rightness in making personal choices in interests of common wellbeing — what are moral choices of conscience. Conscience is the action faculty of worthy (sacra) purpose (mens) — Sacrament.

In experiencing the trajectory of evolution (wave/ particle dynamics) we get the sense that everything is an "arrow in flight," always forward tending and future directed; sin is the arrow falling short of its target. The energy of projection is wave/ particle impulsion. Personal experience and wave/ particle consciousness tell us that everything MUST change, and everything IS changing — the point of birth/ death, the seasons of life, and the ascendancy of consciousness.

Because transformation is the inner compulsion of wave/ particle purpose, as disposed in the symbiotic forms of life, we know that the complexity of life's purposes changes as life's stages self-advance. It flies in the face of reality to freeze life in status-quo mindsets. The dynamic of necessary transformation reveals to us the meaning of and the reality of "Eucharist," namely, that all soul/ substance is together compelled toward newness from within by the common dynamic in all "otherness." We are not today what we were yesterday, we are not now what we were a moment ago; even as you read, you are changing. The inner compulsion of everything to change from within is the mystery of Universal Eucharist.

The impulsive necessity of inner purpose toward ascendancy into higher self-realization is a reach of consciousness toward ultimacy, toward "Godlikeness." Eucharist is the conscionable, purposeful virtue of seeking to understand and be Godlike to the extent humanly possible; it is a spiritual restlessness that pursues the higher purposes of divinity in the giving of self over to the transformation of otherness. The consciousness of divinity impels, compels all reality in Eucharistic purpose. DIVINITY is the love-quest behind Moral Imagination, the mystical faculty of personal/ cultural unity/ continuity, the celebratory "Mass of the Universe." (Chardin)

Falsely Informed Worldview

A dogma is only as true as the worldview from which it comes. Truth cannot be premised in falsehood. Static-centrism, the worldview source of Scholastic Theology/ Ecclesiology is misinformed in story, justification and culture; the cult of hierarchical overreach subsumes personal authenticity and inflicts cumulative catastrophe on people and Earth. Is there no escape from cultic religion, its falsehoods and the suffocation of personal authenticity? except for the potential of reason and faith, no. This indicates the urgency of humankind at this time to wake up to the hopeful insights of personal faith and reason and the resolution of global crises.

Hiding from Learning

People are selective in what they want to learn. And sometimes they screen out what they don't want to learn so that their beliefs and comforts aren't disturbed. The hierarchy of cultic religion seems in the least uninterested if not wholly dismissive of learning evolution-science since its insights might challenge the "truths" by which they live.

Institutional churches have a lot to be embarrassed about, for if they admit the deception and incredibility of the static-centrist worldview they in effect admit the errors of past thinking that wrongfully presume on credibility. A theology that presumes the infallibility of the faith it requires understandably trembles if it is challenged by exposure of error in its teaching and structure. Surely, the connection of cultural inauthenticity (institutional) to fixated theological/ moral underpinnings is obvious.

The free flow of information today and the inroads of scientific understanding challenge status-quo thinking. People are becoming more informed, especially in the sciences and cannot help but question misinformed faith of past culture. Churches and clerics are expected to be faithful to truth even if it requires growth in thinking and belief.

Learning can be scary, because if we are honest with truth, new knowledge may force us to change our ways. This truth exposes the complacency of "people of faith" who do not want to learn about science and evolution. Institutions are threatened also; it's hard to accept truths that shatter structural complacency and highly regarded mythologies. People increasingly and rightly question faith still captured by static-centrist thinking.

It serves patriarchal advantage to treat adults as children and to keep their faith childishly shallow. As long as people remain childish in faith understanding they are more easily held captive; but when adult awareness wakes up to institutional shallowness, people are likely to "lose" faith. More correctly, it's not that they "lose" faith so much as that they discover ownership of faith and the need to be open to growth and not boxed in by institutional presumption.

The Second Vatican Council recognized prevailing global desperation and institutional failing. Circular faith held within a closed loop of repetitive tradition isn't really faith rather it is fideism for it first serves institutional interest rather than people-interest. The updating of faith and reason together is the only way that faith preserves and serves authentically, and is credibly renewed in every generation. [Second Vatican Council, Constitution IV, Gaudium et spes, Intro, #5]

People — God's "Stewards" on the Land

The recognition of stewardship is good, but not adequate. Understanding of stewardship connects with the parable of the talents, of the master who turned over to others money to be invested while he was away. Stewardship implies taking care of something not belonging to oneself, something outside oneself. The problem with "stewardship" is failure to recognize that nature, ecology, is not outside our self, it is the very soul, the stuff of our self.

Because we are religiously cultured in dualism, we misunderstand the essential "insideness" of our personal nature; NATURAL ORGANIC LIFE IS OUR VERY OWN BEING. We belong to God because we belong to God's Creation. Human life is sustainable only as long as organic life is sustainable. Rightly understood, the admonition to be good stewards is an admonition to love nature as we love our selves and to care for nature as we take care for ourselves. The alienation of women in religious culture is of a piece with cultural disconnection of the human self from its essential nature. Stewardship is inadequate because it presumes dualism. http://www.gather.com/viewArticle.action?articleId=281474977542405

39

We are pretentious and self-deceiving when we take a "righteous" stand against human abortion but are at the same time totally indifferent to the abortion of natural ecologies caused by mindless exploitation, pollution and waste of nature.

OTHERNESS — Eucharistic Realism/ Altruism

The "moral commons" is the altruistic realization of "Eucharistic" otherness. The need of global religion and culture for ENLIGHTENMENT and REFORMATION is ongoing and especially urgent now, for the wasting of the "moral commons" is greater today than ever before.

Any morally credible politician or religious leader will seek to awaken grassroots commitment to restore and secure the symbiotic base of nature. Civil society, enlightened religion/ politics together depend on the realism/ altruism of symbiotic codependency — the "Moral Commons."

At issue globally is the lethal competition between "soft energy" (diverse symbiosis) and "hard energy" (fossil fuels and nuclear fusion/ fission.) Hard-energy exploitation trashes the soft energy "ecos." Sustainable life and the future of humanity depend on Nature's soft-energy management of hard energy.

SO LET'S FACE IT

When it comes to the overlooked and cumulative debt of human exploitation imposed on nature, we, the people, are as conflicted as politicians with the global debt crises. As natural resources are running out, so is time for humankind to reverse its runaway exploitation of Nature.

Self-interest politics trumps moral imagination when it comes to corporate capitalism's mindless exploitation of Nature. Enlightened politics is needed not just for dealing with the American debt crisis but also for dealing with the moral crisis of the Commons. The economic bankruptcy of nations has blood ties to global ecological bankruptcy. Mindless human consumption of nature conjures up the repulsive image of maggots consuming a dead carcass. Enlightenment isn't redeemed except religion is redeemed at the same time.

http://www.gather.com/viewArticle.action?articleId=281474978 251339

Global ecological degradation is aggravated by greed for corporate profiteering on life's necessities. For-profit marketing of hard-energy and energy-intensive agriculture, the trashing of bioregional diversity, the global explosion of human populations, and conflicted religious ideologies are all conspiring to create the perfect storm of global collapse.

Solution? Recognizing the global plight of the Moral Commons and its human causes, is a beginning. Massive hands-on human work, less dependency on fossil fuels, is needed bioregionally to restore and sustain natural diversity. Religious collaboration across ideological divides is the Enlightenment needed to give real substance to what religion, Eucharistic realism means. The trashing of the God/ Land/ Human Covenant exposes religion's failed sense of and commitment to Eucharist.

Divinity vs. Empire

It is hard to conceive any two more contrasting and incompatible realities than that of Godlikeness and imperial likeness. This is especially so for Christianity which claims its name from the person of Jesus, the Christ (the anointed one), whom it models as the compassionate exemplar of self "serving the interests and wellbeing of others." And yet, Roman Imperialism succeeded in co-opting Christianity by subsuming it to conform to its way of thinking (politics) and operating (structure). Roman Catholicism persists to the present time in imperial theology (thinking) and ecclesiology (operating).

In his lifework, and in his dying, Jesus stood against the Temple and Empire which together acted explicitly to destroy him because of the threat he was to them. Twenty centuries later, how have competitive divinity and empire fared? Christianity yet conforms to the subsumed likeness of empire as in the time of Constantine. Imperial modeling is evident in the guilt-and-fear method of control and the imposition of faith expectations on the people. Arguably, because of the persistent imperial overreach of Christianity, Christianity has not yet been practiced in the Jesus vision much less has Jesus' vision been culturally embraced or experienced. Institutional Christian denominations to this day are yet duped in the fraud of imperial history and culture, and the compassionate good news of Jesus has been distorted to fit the schemes and scams of temple and empire.

Really, how different are today's church hierarchy from the Scribes and Pharisees of the Temple of Jesus' time? Like them, church hierarchy today makes exclusive claim of authority in matters of faith and morals, even as their example is a public scandal. In view of imperial shamelessness and hierarchical arrogance, how different are they? Really! To the candid observer, they are not at all that much different.

In some ways modern church "scribes and pharisees" are perhaps even less respectable in view of their calculated alienation of women from equal roles in church, but also for their tolerance for and cover-up of sexual predation and abuse by clerics. Eucharistic Altruism is frustrated by the overreach and violation of women by hierarchy at all levels. Most responsible is the Curial structure put in place in imitation of the Imperial Roman Curia. Eucharist, Sacraments are about holy, mindful living in the sacred reality of nature; they are not imperial theatre.

Choosing Hell or Happy

At the very depth of wave/ particle resonance, we belong to the quantum-electric universe and it belongs to us. Reflective consciousness is qualified in the dynamics of plus-minus electrical tension; electrical like-charges repel, whereas, unlike charges attract and open links to convergence and emergence.

The hyper-charged potentials at opposite poles are batteries of energy that open creativity when grounded by discharge. The grounding of self-reflection is an emergent qualification of electrical discharge even as is the drive of evolution. But, creativity does not always work benignly; schizophrenia, for example, is the conflicted back-talk of dualistic dissonance that rattles the brain — the "devil" within.

Charges at opposite poles can be thought of as the dynamic between the divine and the diabolical (satanic). The diabolical is the hyper-charge of mono-polarity, whereas, the divine is the convergence of harmony that opens potentials of emergence and discharges the hyper-charge of dissonance. In nature, lightning flashes signal the grounding (discharge) of polar hyper-charge, even as occurs more subtly at the micro-level in/ between neurons.

Conflicted energies are at work in resonance and dissonance. Hyper tensions characterize the overload of polarized charges in people, in men and women. Excess negative charge (electrons) characterizes male dissonance, and excess positive charge (positrons) characterizes female dissonance. Harmonic energy radiates in the grounded activation of plus-minus charges converging with impregnation as in the sexual analogy. Openness to the mutuality of other is "heaven";

the hyper culture of ego insulates self from mutuality with other and sets up hellish conflicts.

No need to look beyond the conscious self for devils; they already abound in each of us. But not to be discouraged, if the enemy is within, so is the friend. The experience of natural grace is in the mutual grounding of tensions of hyper-charge. "Trimorphism" is the process of resonance, but also of dissonance at work in the purgatory (jihad) of consciousness coming to human realization. Trimorphic Resonance characterizes the divine and "trimorphic dissonance" characterizes the diabolical. Divine Trinity is reflected in the resonance of communication (trust), consciousness (hope) and conscience (love); satanic trinity is oppositely characterized in the dissonance of ignorance (distrust), arrogance (self-obsession) and greed (quest of surfeit). The contest of resonance and dissonance goes on within.

Dissonant voices within conflict consciousness and obstruct relationships. The resonance of convergent consciousness enables bonding and the construction of relationships. Ego-centric consciousness strikes out against the equal affirmation of other and frustrates the potentials of relationships. The grounding of faith/ reason (female/ male mutuality) enables potentials of emergence to overcome closed polarity. Grounding happens in the dialog of faith and reason, woman and man; grounding is the beginning of "happy", resonant harmony.

http://www.gather.com/viewArticle.action?articleId=2814749784 59272

A Hurting World

We live in a hurting world and we all suffer the world's hurt. Hurt doesn't just happen, it is caused. And until we understand the causes of world hurt, there isn't much chance that we can mitigate hurt and facilitate healing.

Chances are that as persons of a hurting world, we are hurting now. But, does that mean that our lives are forever defined by hurt and that we have no hope of rising above it? Yes, in real ways we are defined by hurt, but we are not fated to be defined by it nor are we consigned to hopelessness and despair.

The reality of hurt cannot be escaped, whether for reasons of mindlessness, willfulness or ignorance; by these we are hurt and we cause hurt. So, how can we take control of our lives and mitigate our own hurt and minimize the hurt we cause others? by removing mindlessness, willfulness and ignorance from our lives.

Mindlessness: we need to come to terms with ourselves as to how and why we are hurting, and how and why we hurt others. Mindfulness requires awareness in the moment of our motives in choices we make, and their consequences.

Willfulness: if we are angry and vindictive, we harbor within ourselves diseased ideas that aggravate hurt and prevent our own healing. This violence in ourselves breaks out in violence toward others. If we let our hurt drive us to vengeance, to "get even" with others, there can be no healing — only more hurt. How can we stop the cycle of violence? by compassion for ourselves and others — and for the transformational necessity that defines life in the iteration cycles of birth-death, birth-death, on and on. Compassion, as in Eucharistic mindfulness/ purpose, is the only solution.

Ignorance: Ignorance is intellectual blindness; knowledge is light, the clarification of insight. Knowledge of the causes of hurt can open us to getting beyond our own hurt and hurting others. The pursuit of Word, Light and Love, by way of communication/ consciousness/ conscience, is the way we overcome ignorance and exercise mindfulness.

Re-Membering Sacred Things

The word SACRAMENT means "sacred remembrance" — and the process of intentional agency in remembering sacred things. All of nature is sacred because of ever-present "divine instance." Vitality is about "re-membering," psychically, physically.

It is in the order of nature (femaleness) to re-member; the evolved mechanism of two sexes (female-male) is the enabling basis of higher consciousness. In the higher order of consciousness the two sexes are mutually complementary and co-essential.

In the natural order of sacred remembrance, the sequence of connection is: evolution, biology and theology. Except for evolution, there is no biology, no theology. The higher order of consciousness could not be except for the lower foundational orders of evolution and biology.

Evolution is the working agency that gives memory connection (DNA) to sacred existence (divine instance), and is the essential process and precondition of the continuing work of biology (web-life connections) and theology (conscionable reflectivity.) Faith grounds in evolution; hope grounds in life; and love grounds in theological consciousness — Trimorphic Resonance.

C'mom hierarchy! C'mon Pope Benedict! Get in the game of life and rise above cultural ignorance and arrogance. Don't be spooked by the word evolution; just start mouthing it, and eventually you will catch on and get in the flow of life's ongoing process of re-membering

Is Culture too Institutionally Beholden?

In matters of religion, it's as if only institutions matter. Priorities need to be re-ordered. Institutions suppose people; religion supposes people. As to religion, institutions treat laity as aliens. For example, a writer has standing only if institutionally acknowledged.

Non-institutionally accredited writers are non-entities in so far as institutions are concerned.

If I belonged to a religious institution and wrote what I write and got it published, I probably would gain the notoriety of being excommunicated. Because I'm not institutionally connected, my writings get no institutional notice. I continue to deal with institutional disregard. Sometimes I think "I should be so lucky to be excommunicated and have my writings publicly condemned." www.secondenlightenment.org, www.evolution101.org, www.divinicom.com

Church's Self-Delegitimization

A broad-stroke review of hierarchical activity from 1965 to the present time gives the laity a distinct sense that the episcopacy has been radically corrupted from within and the People of God have been radically defrauded.

The revelation of church fallibility and corruption "from within" occurred in the context of drafting and issuing the Humanae Vitae Encyclical. Arthur Jones coined an apt phrase that describes this sorry happening, "the dawn of the Wojtyla-Ratzinger continuum." ["The Roman Imposition," The NATIONAL CATHOLIC REPORTER, Vol. 41, No. 39, pp. 7&8, September 9, 2005; Sylvester L Steffen, "Woman in a Shoe," Appendix B, pp. 45&46, THE POSSIBLE JOURNEY, UNCOMPROMISED TRUST]

http://www.authorhouse.com/Bookstore/BookDetail.aspx?Book=257970

In drafting the encyclical Humanae Vitae, Pope Paul VI convened a panel of laity to provide input, consistent with the legitimate authority of laity in Church. However, in evaluating the lay contribution, Pope Paul VI was persuaded to issue the encyclical "clean" of lay input. Ever since, and with justification, laity have insistently and consistently rejected Humanae Vitae, not only because of the overt clerical snub of the laity by Rome but also because of clerical prejudice adverse to female/ male equivalency.

The papacy of John Paul II pursued his determination to reject other essential aspects of the Second Vatican Council, specifically, Liberation Theology, by electing bishops and cardinals who favored Tridentine Theology/ Ecclesiology over Vatican II Theology/ Ecclesiology. Pope Benedict XVI (Joseph Cardinal Ratzinger, Prefect of the "Congregation for the Doctrine of the Faith" under Pope John Paul II) continues in his papacy with the Wojtyla-Ratzinger project to delegitimize The Second Vatican Council and return to disciplines of the First Vatican Council and Tridentine Theology/ Ecclesiology.

What more evidence of "church fallibility" is needed than this imposition on the people, conspired and executed in the course of the last 55 years? One can only hope that this matter receives priority attention.

COMMUNION, Process not Stasis

The "Communion of Saints" is process, not stasis, even as is Trinity and the vitalizing breath of the Holy Spirit (Ruach, the ground-state of femininity.) It is in process that we individually come to discover self-identity in communion. The trustworthy foundation and authentic means of communion are faith, hope and love, advanced and authenticated by trustworthy communication, informed consciousness and committed conscience.

As process and as community, all the faithful are necessarily implicated and involved in Communion. Process of communion is the ongoing pursuit of harmony not the mindless repetition of rote platitudes brought forward in the incestuous orthodoxy of medieval construed dogma, but in vital enlightenment of theology and ecclesiology consistent with the fresh air of evolved insights based on updated science and it implications to natural/ human/ divine relationships. There is no hope and no future in returning to the dualistic presumptions of Trent and Vatican I.

Is the present company of bishops likely to go against the current of recidivism put in place by Popes John Paul II and Benedict XVI? Not likely. The waters of Vatican II have been soured by official church in its intentional complicity/ conspiracy, and until there are new bishops and cardinals who admit to this sour conspiracy and are truly open to the Communion of Saints, including the live laity of today, female and male, there will be no change.

Communal trinity, harmonized in the processes of "Trimorphic Resonance," communication (faith), consciousness (hope), and conscience (love), needs to be at work in persons and in church, not the "antithetical trinity" of unenlightened ignorance, dogmatic arrogance and obsession in primacy stasis. Vatican II gave rise to the Spirit of Hope that communal harmony can happen — and the People Church will not give up on the Spirit of Hope.

Maleness derives from Femaleness

The truism of Metagenesis states: "the SPOROPHYTE is borne as a PARASITE on the ARCHEGONIUM of the GAMETOPHYTE."

SPOROPHYTE is: a spore producing plant. All land plants, and some algae, have life cycles in which a haploid gametophyte generation alternates with a diploid sporophyte; PARASITE is: a host-dependent, attached organism; ARCHEGONIUM is: "arche" means, primary, beginning, from Greek; and"gonium" means a cell that produces reproductive cells; GAMETOPHYTE is: multicellular phase of plants and algae that undergo alternation of generations, haploid-diploid, female-male (see Wikipedia definitions).

In plain English, the biological truism states that the archegonium produces diploid/ haploid cells, the ovum (female) and the spores (male); "diploid" means full complement of cell-nucleus chromosomes; "haploid" means half the complement of cell-nucleus chromosomes.

Grasses, e.g., corn, are further evolved; the tassel of the corn produces the spores, the ear produces the ova; kernels of corn are formed when spores fertilize the ova. The pollination of many flowering plants depends on insect carriers to bring pollen to the ovum, honeybees, for example.

Seeds are products of diploid/ haploid reproduction; the germ cell of (grasses) corn grain has diploid chromosome content, and so does the corn plant that grows from the seed germ; the mitochondrial DNA and plastid DNA of the seed endosperm are of female origin only. [The DNA contribution of male sperm, for example, is only to the cell (ovum) nucleus, not to plastids or mitochondria, the means of energy metabolism transmitted in female cytoplasm.]

NOW, after putting biology in right order, theological extrapolations can be put in right order, namely, TO CORRECT THE FALSE PRESUMPTION that males are "primary" and females are "secondary." In the real world, it's the other way around.

A synod may be an appropriate forum in which to deal with the crisis of truth and church credibility caused in no small part by the dogmatic culture of ignorance and arrogance. Perhaps for the first time, church might respect the contributions of Pierre Teilhard de Chardin, and show openness to evolution.

Remembering Mother

There's no grief like a smitten mother's. Jesus in his time rebuked the cultic priesthood of the Temple; Church today, like Mary, The Pieta, is deeply grieved over the alienation women suffer at the hands of cultic hierarchy.

Late in life have I awakened to the power of a name and the deep trauma of a mother's grief. My namesake, Pope Sylvester, has until now been unknown to me, and only now I discover some things in common I might have with him. [AMERICA Magazine, May 2-9, 2011, pp. 23, 24, Paul Nienaber's Review of Nancy Marie Brown's "THE ABACUS AND THE CROSS, The Story of the Pope Who Brought the Light of Science to the Dark Ages.] In some ways my religious calling and my passion for science define my life as they did Pope Stlvester's.

Only by unusual circumstance did I come to be named Sylvester, and only my mother knows why. Her preference was to call me Loras after the first bishop of the Dubuque Territory. But the parish priest objected because Loras was not a saint's name. With reluctance and chagrin, and surely with disappointment, she relented.

Has my mother's grief marked me to remind the hierarchy of the grief all women suffer from cultic alienation? Clerics! Think twice before calling a mother's wrath down on yourselves!

ONTOGENY: the Becoming of Being

Why does the sequence of how "being comes to be" matter? because the priority of interdependency determines the authentic hierarchical structuring of organized societies.

If the priority of relationships is wrongly theologized and politicized, so are societies. This is a societal matter of critical concern in the present time because patriarchal culture has presumed for males the role of social priority when in fact maleness is a derived diversification of femaleness, as evolutionary science reveals. The social priority (equality) of females is formally denied in religious culture — a defect that is increasingly problematic as social relationships evolve into ever greater complexity.

"Adam, that is, mankind, has a partner and mate, adamah, land," as

Walter Brueggemann discerned and stated so well, "Humankind and land are thus linked in a covenantal relationship, analogous to the covenantal relationship between man and woman ... unfortunately, in our society we have terribly distorted relationships between man and woman, between adam and adamah, distortions that combine promiscuity and domination.... Likely, we shall not correct one of these deadly distortions unless we correct them both". http://www.gather.com/viewArticle.action?articleId=2814749775 42405

The reality of female priority in evolution exposes the fundamental error of patriarchal religion's (theology) and dominion culture's (ecclesiology,) a problem recognized formally in the Second Vatican Council. (Constitution IV, Gaudium et spes, Introduction, #5, paragraph #4.) Subsequently, Pope John Paul II has spoken to this reality, that is, to the priority of the "Marian" over the "Petrine." See: George Weigel, "Witness to Hope, The Biography of Pope John Paul II," pg. 578: "The Pope also discusses Mary's particular importance for women in terms of the priority of discipleship. If the Marian Church of disciples is 'before' the Petrine Church of office, then there is a fundamental, baptismal equality of discipleship in the Church — between women and men, as well as between laity and clergy — that is prior to any distinction of function."

Ontologically, maleness depends from/on femaleness. The reality of ontological priority changes everything — as Vatican II says, this matter is "as important as can be," as are "new analysis and synthesis" of theology/ ecclesiology premised on ontological understanding of female priority.

At this particular time, as institutional churches, ecologies and economies are mortally hurting, there may be no greater priority than the calling of a new Church Council to correct the disorder that has been in place for millennia.

Women religious and men! Please step forward and urge the

correction and removal of false understandings that yet prevail within the Petrine Church and bedevil world civilizations. More troubling is the present determination of the Petrine Church to return to the theology/ ecclesiology of Trent. The AMERICAN CATHOLIC COUNCIL (q.v.) is a medium calling world attention to the fraudulent premise of male priority in church/ society, and toward the convening a global Catholic Council.

Two quite different Continuities

There are two quite different "continuities" that co-evolved and are at play here. The first is ongoing (Council of Trent) thinking and control over ecclesiology and theology; the second, contemporary with Vatican I, was the shift from Kingdom politics, albeit unwilling, to the Mission of the Gospel of Peace and Justice (Leo XIII), which took place after the Papal States (the Papal Kingdom) were lost.

The second continuity was terminated by action of the Italian government which "liberated" the church from Kingdom status and business; Pope Leo XIII took up the Gospel Mission of Peace and Justice, as did the popes succeeding him, and which was further advanced by the Second Vatican Council.

The continuity mission of the Gospel of Peace and Justice is the hermeneutic that matters for it corresponds with the Christian mandate. But Popes John Paul II and Benedict XVI returned to first continuity thinking and control (Tridentine) that had been updated and modified by the Second Vatican Council. Pope John Paul II enabled serious return to recidivist thinking and control, and frustrated the work of Vatican II by appointing like-minded bishops and cardinals.

Thomas Aquinas' End-of-Life Epiphany

What is most notable in the end-of-life years of the Great Doctor of the Church, St Thomas Aquinas, was his total silence about his writings and his refusal to write any more. This change of life was so unlike his whole prior life that it is obvious he came to an epiphany, and even disdained his writing. The radical alienation of woman from rightful and equal role in the order of nature and in Church is nothing short of being a "radical culture of distrust."

This radical culture of distrust persists to this day and is at the root of women's alienation in church, church's loss of credibility, and the wasteful exploitation of nature. Thomas Aquinas argued in his Summa Theologica the rationale of males (Adam) being primary in the order of creation and females "secondary."

The elaboration of literal belief in Adam-rib-creation of Eve is a metaphor used to state first creation of Adam and the dependent creation of Eve. In the order of spirituality males are presumed more Godlike; females are "inferior" and more corruptible. If the consequences of literal belief were not so tragic, this Story would be laughable in light of postmodern consciousness.

Thomas Aquinas, in the end and to his credit, seems by his epiphany to have come to a whole new understanding of the divine/ human relationship, which made all his other writings seem to him to be so much "straw." The new and over-riding important insight he came to was his sense of Eucharist Altruism and the instance of divinity, at-one-ment in the order of nature and consciousness.

Eucharistic Altruism

Eucharistic altruism is the pinnacle prerogative of sexual purpose, equivalent in woman and man; altruism is the wisdom of putting other before self. The prerogatives of sex are about choice; choice is about the conscionable discernment of better options that depreciates no one but appreciates all.

One of the more astounding things about nature is the wild way nature displays her sexual prerogatives. The exotic displays of sex cut across all species of flora and fauna. This grandeur of natural imagination ranges from strange and wonderful colors and appendages to complex habits that defy logic except for originality. The birds of paradise of New Guinea are hardly excelled by any other creature as to color and pomposity. And the mix of practical and impractical in nest building is the specialty of the bower bird. Then there are fish and amphibians in which the males of some species shield and care for the young in or on their bodies. Males are usually the ones who parade exotic excess to win the favors of the females who for security reasons have the good sense to avoid exotic extravagance.

Nature, symbiosis and Eucharist are of a piece, except that Eucharist, the purposeful giving of self to other, takes on dimensions of self-reflectivity so that ways of giving self to other are more diverse, imaginative and intellectually responsive to changing circumstances in the here and now.

Intelligence is a grade above hard wiring for it is capable of adding purpose and intention to the symbiotic calculus of chemistry. Humankind has the faculty of conscience. The males of the human species seem to have more trouble than females in finding the niche for reason in the weave of faith. The waste of nature is a bitter taste, and we better try harder or the accomplishments of faith will be brought to naught. It is time males parade less pomposity and engage more sensibly. Sensibility compels one to discern the quandary: Is sex a marketable commodity or personal prerogative?

Males have institutionalized marriage and made sex their "right" and woman's "obligation." In effect, the "marriage contract" serves the male conspiracy of imposing on females and nature in valuating sex as a marketable commodity subject to contractual law, thus disconnecting it from what it is, a prerogative of personal identity. If one questions the value males put on sex, consider: a reward promised suicide bombers is virtually unlimited access to virgins in heaven showering sexual favors on the bomber for his self-immolation.

Challenging the rationality of the institutional marriage contract is like striking a wasp's nest and inviting oneself to be stung. But, let's face it, Earth-life is being suffocated because it is over wrought by population appetites beyond the sustainable means of web-ecologies. Males take seriously the self-satisfying mandate "to increase and multiply," but choose to ignore the equally urgent mandate not to consume the fruit of the tree in the middle of the garden (ecological vitality) — the original and ongoing sin of consumptive excess and waste.

For males to institutionalize sex and theology in self-interest is to commercialize (commodify) female graces, what by definition is prostitution. I don't believe God is in the prostitution racket or that heaven is a place of riotous sex, licensed or unlicensed. The culture of male dominion over sex and theology no longer has credibility but has come to a dead end. Evolution Theology is the "wave of the future." http://www.gather.com/viewArticle.action?articleId= 281474979099136

Eucharist and Evolution

EUCHARIST is the process of Divinity becoming Self-reflective in humanity. Humanity is the pinnacle achievement of graced nature. Humanity obtains in and from nature, and in all things, pertains to nature. Self-reflectivity is the high perfection of nature, of the electromagnetic complexity of wave/ particle. All transformation is nature's way of wave/ particle (spiritual/ material) process, the root reality of Eucharistic ascendance in reflective humanity.

The complexity process of wave/ particle is an ascendant process of higher self-reflection, self-perfection, which are processes of Divinity Consciousness, the synthesis of harmonics that gives nature the high purpose of Transcendence into Other. In every aspect of our being, of our consciousness, we obtain from and are caught up in the perpetual transcendence of self-transformation into Other — the essential condition of nature in process — EUCHARISTIC EVOLUTION.

The Great Returning of energy to consciousness, of Divine Instance in ascendant complexity is the restlessness of Love. In the Divine Process of Graced Nature, Eucharistic transformation/ transcendence is Ascendant Evolution into Divinity Consciousness — the Alpha/ Omega of life/ death, the ultimate process of "doing theology," a process Divinely Personal and human — the "Mass of the Universe." (Chardin)

Dark Times for Truth

Deep theology and deep science have evolved esoteric languages and concepts that are generally impenetrable for ordinary folks. Serious but limited effort to penetrate their obscurity has occurred, yet there seems to be a calculated disinterest, perhaps even an arrogant complacency on the part of religion and science to disregard each other's worldview. This disregard damages both.

Sister Ilia Delio, O.S.F., continues to try to change the situation but has been frustrated by unresponsiveness, as have I. My lifetime commitment since 1957 has been to be a go-between for science and religion by learning their languages and concepts and finding correlation between them. In AMERICA Magazine, April 4, 2011, pp. 14-19, she airs her frustration that religious educational institutions (at any level) do not provide a learning forum that seeks correlation of religious/ scientific truths. She writes:

"The mechanization and specialization of higher education has rendered the university a multiversity. Instead of educating students to know the universe and stars "turning together as one," academic disciplines, including theology and philosophy, have become highly specialized, competitive fields. If the modern church is reluctant to embrace insights from modern science as integral to revelation, part of the hesitancy may be due to the place theology holds within the academy...

"Few Catholic theologians are grappling with the sciences on their own terms as a means of theological reflection. While the church recognizes the importance of science for the development of faith, it also recognizes the limits of science as the ultimate horizon of meaning... as theology entered into dialogue with the cultural pluralities of gender, race, history and philosophy, it nonetheless settled into the university system as an academic silo, just as the sciences sequestered themselves into specialized disciplines. Religion and science grew more estranged...

"Scientists tend to see the relationship between the two disciplines as one of either conflict or independence, theologians, when they are interested, tend toward dialogue and integration. Undoubtedly, science and religion are independent disciplines, each with its own language, methods and tools of analysis, but the academic structure has kept them intellectually as well as spatially apart..."

The Evolution Trilogies of this writer present both the esoteric languages and concepts of deep theology and deep science in a way that connects with real life and means something personally and socially. It's not easy but it's important to make religion and science accessible to ordinary folk. GREEN RELIGION (book six) gives a study method that lets readers bite off a little at a time on a daily basis so as to avoid mental indigestion.

While the challenge to lighten religious/ scientific heaviness is difficult, it is important because science and religion need each other's truths to stay relevant. In the long run science will win out if religion chooses to ignore scientific knowledge. Fixation in disconnection is a sure path to irrelevance. Churches are now [at risk of] becoming museums because of the mass exodus of people from them.

The cross-fertilization of religious and scientific jargon produces a new language, and certainly a new worldview. Failure to manage both is a hazard to health and sanity. Mastery begins in home and community, from the bottom up, not from the top down. The correlation of science and religion needs to happen in the earliest years if a person is to grow up comfortable and conversant with both.

IT MIGHT BE ARGUED WITH JUSTIFICATION

that the cultural schism between faith and reason, between materiality and spirituality, is the great tragedy of this time and all time. It's not my intent to make the case for such a sweeping conclusion, but it does serve us well to modestly focus on the beneficial purposes of openness to learn and appreciate the mutual values of faith and reason to each other, and how we might help ourselves in personal living by being more sensitive to interpersonal (religious) relationships within the earthly niche we occupy. Imperial pomposity and institutional hype aside, humankind needs to pursue life's commonalities more humbly.

Biologically and conventionally, cultures represent faith as belonging to the female persona and reason as characteristic of the male persona. The alienation of female from male is driven by the adversarial cultures of faith-suppression and female-exploitation. We are cultured in male hype, dominion, and distrust. The persistent culture of interpersonal alienation widens the rift between faith and reason, between humanity and nature, and between God and man.

The "original" sin of alienation is told in the Garden of Eden story from the perspective of the static-centrist worldview and top-down theology. In the Creation/Fall Story, God gives two commands (1) to increase and multiply and (2) not to consume the vitality-fruit of the Tree of Life. Fast forward to the present time — the global overreach of human population is systemically and globally wasting the Vitality Tree of web-life ecology. The bitter fruit of consuming web-life vitality is global impoverishment and desperation, fueling persistent violence and perpetual warfare.

On Sunday March 20, 2011, Sixty Minutes interviewer Morley Safer visited with Bishop Timothy Dolan of New York (the "American pope"). In the interview Bishop Dolan expressly stated that he and Mr. Safer live in and represent two different and contrasting worldviews, the old world of theological absolutism and the changed world of evolving consciousness.

Contrasting the two worldviews is the perceived fixation of dominion culture in ignorance, arrogance and obsession (greed) as opposed to contemporary openness to communication (faith), consciousness (hope) and conscience (love). Institutional Catholic theology/ ecclesiology holds radically to the Garden of Eden Story, top-down creation, while contemporary consciousness is aware of the inappropriateness of fixation in alienation and corporate exploitation.

Reflective consciousness informs cultural wisdom in the transformational dynamic of "trimorphic resonance", the harmony of WORD-LIGHT-LOVE, of communication, consciousness and conscience. Life on Earth is radically imperiled by self-driven alienation, of females (faith) from males (reason), of humanity from divinity. Global desperation and degradation can only get worse if religion (humankind) persists in the fixations of ignorance, arrogance and obsession.

The radical choice before humankind today is to nurture life or culture pre-mature death; the Godlike affirmative choice is to reject alienation and fixation in division. If we reject fixation in division, we can accommodate the cosmic worldview of evolving consciousness, of transformation, of mutual faith/ reason, and affirm enlightenment. The conflict presented is institutional claim on faith vs. the birthright of joined Faith and Reason.

PUTTING GOD TO THE TEST

At issue is faith, the handed-down wisdom of generations; each generation is the faith-repository of prior wisdom, the agency that acquires new faith, as well as the trustee of wisdom freshly acquired in the ongoing dialog of faith and reason in new experience.

Faith and reason are judge and jury of meritorious new law. The bench of decision is daily in session in every individual conscience; that law endures which consistently passes the conscience-test of time. Law is fine tuned in the court of disciplined thought, "cogitata perficiendo, cogitando sic perfecta" [thinking is perfected in thoroughly thought-through thoughts.]

Law like faith and reason is dynamic, that is, it must speak to the contingencies of the times and adapt to necessities of new experience. The application of old law to new experience isn't always clear and certainly not always easy. Failure of faith to test reason and failure of reason to test faith puts God to the test.

The willful abortion of life is on its face wrong and categorically outlawed, but so is behavior whose cumulative effect is radical abortion. The great moral problem of the time is the overreaching appetite of human populations whose unbridled consumption is having the effect of suffocating nature and extinguishing web-life species critical to human existence.

The outcomes of pollution and exploitation are collapsing live food systems. The moral proportionality of web-life abortion has yet to be considered against the undisciplined interpretation of the Garden mandate to "increase and multiply." Excess of human multiplication (reproduction) has the impact of defeating the successful multiplication of other species; waste and the immoral option of war have yet to be weighed in the religious calculus.

These moral/ practical issues need to be dealt with personally and publicly. A growing awareness of moral judgment is beginning to weigh in, and moral theology is not yet well enough developed to offer settled law. In the meantime, life goes on and people will make radical decisions that may fly in the face of unsettled law (conscience).

Linked to this moral dilemma are issues of gender, the moral justification of same-sex partnerships, issues of family planning and birth control. The crises of conscience are new in every time — which calls for moral sensitivity — for no time-qualified absolute adequately covers all situations.

The formation of personal, conscionable ethics is "situation-based," that is, based on the moral proportionality of outcomes of choice. The seriousness of outcome makes choices all the more difficult — but the responsibility of moral choice cannot be avoided, and best decisions must be made even when the greater good requires the repulsive acceptance of outcomes of lesser evil.

On this issue the eyes of beholders are conflicted. But God leaves to mortals the dilemma of decisions — the weighing of the greater good against the lesser evil. And so, public conflicts will continue, especially when choice might seem to allow one abortion to prevent a perceived more consequential abortion. Even God is tortured by this dilemma. Choosing pregnancy is a moral issue of personal and public concern; let it be a "thoroughly thought-through choice." All life must be valued and nurtured; all are called to be faithful to life as life is faithful to all.

III. LOVE —
the Grace of Conscience

Monotony and Predictability

What in life do you find most monotonous, dull and predictable? What is it about dullness and predictability that makes them monotonous? The root words of monotonous are "mono" and "tone." If we hear one musical chord only — that is monotonous; one song repeated over and over — that is monotonous. If the preaching we hear week-in and week-out is the same — that is monotonous.

I apologize for the monotony of repeating the same themes over and over, but it is necessary to bring to attention non-obvious themes that are controlling in everything we do, but about which we are absent-minded. Out of habit, religious and cultural, we have developed blind spots that filter out consciousness of matters critical to culture and religion. My purpose is to write and repeat the harmonic patterns of intelligence-wisdom by which we are enabled to understand and approach Godlikeness. My object is to lay out a way of owning self-reflection — Eucharist — and coming to compassion and self-fulfillment.

We might think that repetitions of fractal iterations in Earth ecology would be monotonous, deadening — not so — they in fact give continuity and diversity to Earth creativity and vital diversity. Iterative patterns of sustainability underlie all symbiotic relationships, including matters governing human wellbeing. These I have framed in the resonance patterns of communication, consciousness, conscience — INTELLIGENCE; and, faith, hope, love, — WISDOM — themes that I shamelessly repeat, again and again.

Until now, we as the inheritors of nature's graces are all but ignorant of the fundamental tools of consciousness, of spiritual ascendancy. We need to learn and to take ownership of our place and way in the Sacrament of Natural Order.

"Generations of Faith" Inheritance

Faith is the birthright consciousness of human/ divine understanding, otherwise called hypostasis; as such it enlightens justified living. Eucharistic Altruism is life's ultimate justification; willingly or unwillingly, justified living claims all life. We exist not just for ourselves but for other; Eucharistic Altruism leads to other-mindfulness. The fulfilled life embraces Eucharistic Altruism and ultimate justification. Justification is the fulfilled way of life if we but commit ourselves to mindfulness in-the-moment.

By genetic inheritance we possess an inner and evolving compulsion toward fair-mindedness — what enables fulfilled living for oneself and other; the medium of self-reflectivity is organic relationship. Right relationship necessarily links to right-mindedness, to moral consciousness (religion), if we but commit to mindfulness in-the-moment. We inherit the capacity to be "religious" (as concerned for others as we are for ourselves); and by the nurture of culture, community and family, we are helped personally to be religious. Moral imagination enlightens justified living and enables family and community to flourish by way of mutuality, complementarity and subsidiarity.

Moral imagination develops within self-reflective consciousness and is nurtured by communal/inter-personal harmony. The pursuit of inter-communal fulfillment satisfies the individual, female and male, and the community, by way of justified living. Eucharistic altruism is the pinnacle prerogative enabling justified living.

All life is more alike than different. Life evolves genetic means of accomplishing diversification and fulfillment; both are accomplished simultaneously and generationally. Within individual cells are chains of ribonucleic acids, (the nucleotides, A adenine, G guanine, T thymine, and C cytosine) that make up the DNA helix (deoxyribonucleic acid). The DNA helix characteristically governs all life, all genetic transformation, individual diversification and fulfillment. This applies equally to microorganisms, to plant and animal life. Higher life organisms do not reinvent energy-mechanisms rather they incorporate original genetic structures and mechanisms into evolving, symbiotic modifications. For example, the metabolic cell structures of mitochondria and plastids have their individual DNA modified from earlier microbial organisms. [See, Monica Steffen, "The Evolution of Symbiosis", QUANTUM RELIGION, book two of the Evolution Trilogies, pp. 117-123]

Lower life forms are food for higher life forms; human life is unsustainable except the interactive webs of interdependent life are sustained. Complexity consciousness, the ability to be reflective, to engage moral imagination in sorting things out in ways that make sense, are consequences of evolved genetic sequencing. Gene-sequencing has enabled genetic mapping and understanding of functions of genes and the cortical brain.

The internal neurological communication system of the body is the intuitional network of consciousness and of the reflective ability to be morally, mindfully alert in-the-moment. Potentials of psychological growth in genetic mindfulness are only beginning to be understood; their religious significance has hardly entered religious thinking as of yet. The reflectivity of moral imagination has a lot of work to do to catch up with and correct for the cumulative havoc of global bungling.

It was in the decade of the 1950s that my moral imagination woke up and challenged the faith of my upbringing. Faith, like all consciousness, evolves as reason evolves and takes us to unpredictable places. I cannot tell you where your moral imagination will take you, but it is likely that moral imagination will take you to places quite beyond where you are today. The journey beckons anew daily.

As an inducement to encourage others to pursue the quest of moral imagination, all I can do is put before you where the quest has taken me.

WHAT DOES FAITH MEAN TO ME? I believe in justified living, in "mindfulness in-the-moment," pursuing what trust of self and other means in sustaining moral relationships. Morality is personal before it becomes communal, institutional.

WHAT IS "JUSTIFIED LIVING?" Justified living is the product of moral imagination, of proving every choice, every decision by the process of personal/ communal communication – dialogue; consciousness – discernment; conscience - decision.

WHAT FUTURE FAITH-EXPECTATION DO I HAVE? I have the expectation that by fidelity to interpersonal relationships, one and all are inspired by, and inspire others to the expectation of better things to come (HOPE) not just for others but for nature's ecological networks, now and into the future. I expect Generations of Faith to continue to enrich the inheritance value of faith by mindfulness in-the-moment.

The inheritance of moral imagination is ascendant consciousness justified in the processing of "Faith and Reason Together" by way of TRIMORPHIC RESONANCE —faith and reason together in the mindful harmony of communication-dialogue, consciousness-discernment and conscience-decision.

Fundamentalism's "Left Behind" Fixation

Our times are flavored with the apocalyptic novelty of a spate of "Left Behind" books and the G. W. Bush Administration's "No-Child-Left-Behind" agendum. The joined apocalyptical obsessions of the Christian Religious Right and the Republican Party have created a political reality that leaves everyone behind. The report card on education is in: it is failing critical thinking. Education and indoctrination are not the same things, one challenges intelligence while the other dumbs down intelligence by imposing on people faith expectations of authoritarian religion/ government.

http://globaldebateblog.blogspot.com/2011/01/usa-students-fail-to-learn-critical.html

Early Christian fear of Apocalypse focused people on what they believed was the imminent Second Coming of Jesus and end-time. This fixation was a problem for Paul of Tarsus because the people stopped doing normal work-a-day activities, thinking life on Earth would soon be ending, so why bother. Repeatedly Paul insisted the people get back to work so life could go on. Focus on Second Coming as the signal event of end-time lives on in Christianity and remains a definitive aspect of Christian belief today. And there are fundamentalists who now see end-time, Second Coming, just around the corner.

A current of rationality called Gnosticism was present in early Christianity but was suppressed after Bishop Irenaeus and fellow bishops took exception to the proliferation of Christian writings (the Apocrypha). The bishops gave themselves the prerogative of determining what writings would be included in the canon of scriptures. Gnostic scriptures were excluded. Nevertheless, such concepts as Trinity Godhead include elements of Gnostic wisdom, for example, Trimorphic Protennoia.

In our times the decline of critical thinking seems to be in direct proportion to the rise of the Religious Right. The convergence of "Left-Behind" theology, Rightist Republican politics and failure of critical thinking are more than coincidental — they are of a piece. What they don't appreciate is that education isn't about indoctrination; it's about critical thinking, updating collective wisdom, anticipating and providing for the common good. Failed critical thinking is a problem in public schools as much as in church schools. Christian evangelism is weighted toward faith indoctrination from its beginnings. When society fails in critical thinking it fails people, culture, common wellbeing and religion.

Failure of critical thinking has personal and social consequences. Non-critical thinking is culturally integrated when people uncritically accept the fideistic doctrine of institutions, i.e., old beliefs handed down through hierarchical succession. In cultic faith practice the same presumptions that first shaped doctrine in early times are presumed to apply for all time. The 2000-year-old presumptions of faith that worked in earlier times are presumed to work for all times, as if nothing changes; evolutionary experience to the contrary, exposes the lie of fixated cultic presumption.

Critical thinking deals with ongoing acquisitions of knowledge, and application of knowledge to belief and behavior. The expansion of knowledge calls for adjustments to once workable belief, and requires changes from belief and behavior premised in false presumptions. Worldview determines dogma; dogma determines faith expectation. A foundationally changed worldview requires adjustment of faith and dogma. Uncritical belief in the static-centrist worldview, for example, is without credibility in light of evolving worldview understandings of nature. Modern day crises require critical thinking as never before, as well as movement from cultic faith fixation to informed faith evolution; at issue are the viability of natural ecologies and human survival.

A Quantum Leap toward Cultural Reconciliation

The AMERICA Magazine Editorial "Religious Freedom 2011", Jan 24-31, 2011, pg. 5, refers to Pope Benedict XVI's 2011 World Day of Peace address in which he makes a compelling call for religious freedom beyond the stale rhetoric that characterizes evangelical retro-culture in dogmatic fixation.

The editors present the premise of the Pope's message "that without religious freedom men and women cannot develop their own identities in relation to the transcendent horizons that are essential to being human." They quote Pope Benedict that freedom of religion "allows us to direct our personal and social life to God, in whose light the identity, meaning and purpose of the person are fully understood."

"The alternative," the pope continues, "when it is not all-out totalitarianism, is a society that subjects persons to arbitrary political manipulation." Case in point is the capture in recent years of the Republican Party (or is it the other way around) by the Religious Right.

The right of religious freedom includes "the right to change one's faith—to convert—and even the right to profess no religion at all. It welcomes religious pluralism; it affirms the need for public authorities to defend religious minorities; and it encourages interreligious dialogue between religions and cultural institutions." The Pope points out how religious liberty is subverted and defectively advanced: "Religious fundamentalism and secularism are alike; both represent extreme forms of a rejection of legitimate pluralism and the principle of secularity," and both absolutize "a reductive and partial vision of the human person, favoring in the one case forms of religious integralism and, in the other, of rationalism… each person must be able freely to exercise the right to profess and manifest , individually or in community, his or her own religion or faith, in public and in private, in teaching, in practice, in publications, in worship and in ritual observances."

The editors observe, "Such an expansive defense of religious liberty is most welcome in a church that until a half-century ago (Vatican II) supported religious establishment and asserted that error has no rights." This clarion declaration can be read as endorsement for the religious right of women to make their communal decisions in equal standing with men in regard to Eucharistic celebration; men have no right to deny equal standing of women in any matter of religion, including their right to ordination.

The Pope's inclusive scope is for greater reconciliation not only within the church but between and among churches; it is inspiring, breath-taking and definitely encouraging. The acknowledgement of religious freedom is a requisite understanding to dampening the hot rhetoric that rages between the sexes inside churches and amongst religions. Give harmony a chance to bring peace. The catholic cafeteria is now open to the global public. Spirituality and secularity have equal setting at the table.

CHURCH: Infallible or Conciliar?

Institutional Catholicism's intentional political entanglement, over some 1500 years, in imperial politics and church domain expansion have poisoned cultures in their understandings of religious authenticity, and have caused all manner of internal roiling from the grief of cultured inauthenticity.

Church turmoil today roots in medieval power-quests. The Princes of church and kingdoms came from the same families. In early times the competition within imperial kingdoms worked to church advantage because while divided kingdoms vied against each other in their interests, religion was one and the same in all kingdoms, Roman Catholicism. Notable historical coincidences and conflicts in medieval times charged cultures with violent antagonisms and passed them on from generation to generation without resolution; this inheritance in our time is seriously problematic in our time, i.e., the almost unchallenged primacy claim of Roman Catholicism.

Setting the stage for the Crusades, popes garnered an army of their own, the Knights Templar, from within the kingdoms, thus having the human and financial resources available to them to prosecute wars of Crusades at the expense of the kingdoms for religious self-serving purposes. Papal Crusades intended land conquest, the suppression of Islam, and political control over the Holy Land. Over several hundred years under this situation, the kingdoms became degraded in resource and soul due to the church militancy. The accommodation that had evolved between the Eastern Church and Islam was wrecked, which set the stage for reconquest by Islam and a terrible and lasting tragedy for the Eastern Church.

Coincidentally, a growing internal schism between conciliarist ecclesiology and infallibilist ecclesiology was getting intense. It came to the point that two papacies were in existence at the same time, one, which was conciliarist inclined, took residence in Avignon while the papacy in Rome was staunchly infallibilist. The conflict is still not resolved. While infallibilism was the mind of Vatican I and is the mind of the present papacy, conciliarism was strongly favored in Vatican II, and continues to gain credibility.

After the Crusades, popes continued to use the Kingdoms to enforce public conformity to church dogma; "heretics" were prosecuted, tortured and put to death under state auspices on behalf of Roman Catholicism. The witch-craze spread, women were accused of consorting with devils, ignominiously tortured and unjustly put to death. [The history of these critical events is detailed in the book "RELIGION & CIVILITY, the Primacy of Conscience."

http://www.authorhouse.com/Bookstore/BookDetail. aspx?Book=242904

The bottom line is that today's global cultures are so changed from times when church run rough-shod over people, that the survival of medievalism in church tradition is judged as irrational and culturally damaging. The church now has no state resources upon which it can rely to prosecute its infallibilism, so people can take their stand against ecclesial irrationality without fear of torture and death. What seems likely is that the credibility of conciliarism will continue to gain ascendancy while infallibilism will continue to lose credibility. Future church will be very different, perhaps split three ways: a small cultic, infallibilist church in the mode of Trent and Vatican I; an open Vatican II church, conciliarist in its hegemony; and a far larger body of people,Christian in faith but extra-institutional in faith-practice — all of which might be avoided if accommodation between conciliarism and infallibilism can be found. This is certainly the outcome that best serves the commonweal.

The TRUTH about Church Fallibility

Today's building seismic pressures within Roman Catholicism are a consequence of a long train of sorry and tragic coincidences which occurred during and since the Middle Ages, all of which are entanglements of the church's own making. These entanglements are about the conflicted positions as to whether church authority is or should be conciliar, i.e., collegial and involving the whole people, or, wholly invested in papal infallibility.

The fraudulent use of the Sacrament of Confessional in prosecuting heretics and in extracting confessions from women of consorting with devils, and the official church requirement of the confessional secret, even in the covering up of clerical sexual abuse, are damaging exposures of the top-down lie of infallibility. This sorry history is detailed in the book "RELIGION & CIVILITY, The Primacy of Conscience." http://www.authorhouse.com/Bookstore/BookDetail. aspx?Book=242904

See also, http://www.ncronline.org/blogs/just-catholic/coming-american-schism

TRUTH Changes Everything

If I were to write a letter to Pope Benedict XVI (and the bishops), this is what I would tell them, "truth liberates from the bondage of error."

The presupposition that the female person derives physically and psychologically from the male, and is therefore beholden (secondary) to him in everything, is a given of patriarchal faith culture as advanced from literal belief in the Garden of Eden Mythology.

Evolution history reveals that sexual distinction was by way of the metagenetic process in which "femaleness" reproduced its kind by cell division and the inside cellular encoding of DNA. DNA coding evolved complexity mechanisms of female origin that brought about greater genetic mixing of phenotypical and genotypical traits by way of separating gametes (female and male), insuring greater mixing of difference.

The truth of informed evolution trumps the false presumption of "religious" history. Walter Brueggemann is right in his assessment: "Adam, that is, mankind, has a partner and mate, adamah, land. Humankind and land are thus linked in a covenantal relationship, analogous to the covenantal relationship between man and woman ... unfortunately, in our society we have terribly distorted relationships between man and woman, between adam and adamah, distortions that combine promiscuity and domination.... Likely, we shall not correct one of these deadly distortions unless we correct them both". [Bernard Evans & Gregory Cusack, Editors, "The Theology of Land", 1987, The Liturgical Press, Collegeville, Minnesota]

http://www.gather.com/viewArticle.action?articleId=2814749775 42405

Water is Primary, Oil is Secondary

"Cosmic Ordination" is an evolving process, an ascendant refinement of self-conscious life, derived in water, cosmically ordained and cosmically confirmed in the oil of DNA.

Ordination and Confirmation are derived awarenesses; they are "secondary" to "Baptismal" consciousness — even as Pope John Paul II affirms that the "Petrine" is secondary to the "Marian."

Amniotic Divinity Consciousness is primary even as self-reflection evolves in Conscious Light. Photo-electric consciousness is photosynthetic awareness in Divine Food, Daily Bread, the sustaining construct of Divine Instance, present to life in the "Naturalis Sacramentum Ordinis."

Divine Instance in the Sacrament of Natural Order is the Universal (Cosmic) Bread of Life, the Panis Angelicus. In the Sacrament of Natural Order, we are bread to one another. We live by Divine Presence; we consume Divine Presence, we are consumed in/ by Divine Presence.

In the "Process of Trinity", the Process of Word, Eucharist, femininity is the primacy consciousness of Divinity Presence in whom arises the ascendant Word of conscious Self-reflectivity. "Memento homo quia pulvus es, et in pulverem reverteris." We are HUMUS, the rooting ground of life.

The Trinitarian Antithesis

Evildoing is a proclivity we all carry within ourselves; it's in the nature of incompleteness, and it roots in perception, in instinctive fixity. In some manner or other, all evil, personal and institutional, roots in ignorance, arrogance and obsession, the "trinitarian antithesis."

Obsession goes beyond inclination when ignorance and arrogance play on ego-centric sensitivities. Fixation in incomplete and erroneous information is fixation in ignorance and arrogance. Fixation in incompleteness is a failure of faith and reason. When we place self-interest (institutional) above the commonweal (nature), we do violence to ourselves and to the commonweal.

The pursuit of personal/ social authenticity is by way of "faith seeking intelligence, and intelligence seeking faith," the way of overcoming the evil of ignorance in the mutual working of faith/ reason. The mindfulness of Eucharist (necessary transformation into other) is the consciousness that lets us overcome arrogance. Obsession enables ignorance, ignorance enables obsession. Humility, knowledge of the ephemeral nature of life, of Eucharist, is the antidote to arrogance. When the evils of ignorance and arrogance are overcome, so is the evil of obsession and fixation in self.

The decision to fixate knowledge in closed terms is to lock oneself in ignorance and to arrogate presumptions of owning truth and full knowledge of God. This is the fatal sin of pride, the crisis of dominion theology.

The Trinitarian Thesis

Trimorphic Resonance, seeks Godlikeness on a continuing basis, ever updating incomplete knowledge and applying new knowledge to changing experience. Trimorphic Resonance is the co-dependent processing of faith and reason by way of communication, consciousness and conscience, the way of "symbiotic evolution", of vital intelligence.

Like all living organisms, institutions must give way to necessary updating or become irrelevant. Roman Catholicism is still exposed to the mortal risks of arrogance, alienation and irrelevance, if it persists in backward focus and fixation in fideism.

Western and Middle Eastern cultures share the common blood of Abrahamic inheritance. The 7-day Creation Story and the rib-origin of Eve from Adam define the perennial theology/ philosophy of Abrahamic tradition globally. All Christian denominations are infected with the memetic disease of "male myopia."

Consistent with the redemptive message of Jesus, EVOLUTION SCIENCE radically challenges the presumptive dominion culture of Abrahamic Tradition. "Divinity Consciousness", as exemplified and taught by Jesus, The Christ, is the bottom-line paradigm of Godlikeness, of EUCHARIST, intended to redeem global culture and redirect the history of humankind. The children of Abraham have not yet got the message, and all global life is victimized by willful myopia.

Until church opens itself to evolution and admits evolution's relevance to theology and ecclesiology, church cannot reasonably expect people to submit themselves to it. It is wrongheaded to fixate the minds of the faithful in medieval dominionism — more specifically, it is a culpable scandal that violates innocence and rapes nature. There's no return to the past; overdue is the end to culture's scandal of denying evolution.

The Obligation of Personal Conscience

To be personally responsible for everything we do and say is scary. We have been conditioned by institutional religion to let the institution define faith content and control our conscience, so the burden of making conscionable choices is yet largely given over to churches. The personal accountability of faith and reason—faith holding reason accountable and reason holding faith accountable—is lacking in religious culture. Traditional faith has been hyped and the role of reason has been subsumed; this is the bone of contention between dominion theology and Enlightenment, and is an underlying factor in the wars of religions. It's more comforting to let church be our conscience, except, the non-use of cumulative intelligence in the faith equation misinforms faith, reason and reality, and alienates us from one another and from nature.

Earth's network life is desperately degraded and so is humankind because of the habituated culture of the alienation of the sexes and disregard for nature. The culture of false dichotomies, i.e., reason vs. faith; soul vs. body; male vs. female; spirituality vs. materiality; creationism vs. evolution; institution vs. person drives us apart; you get the idea.

Tsunamis of eco-social crises are washing across all global civilizations without regard for people, but as the result of the conscienceless exploitation of nature. Everything has to change, including churches. The failure of personal conscience is at the root of mindless behavior, what has become a culture of desperation.

I know this message is unsettling, but even more unsettling is our failure to be individually responsible for our personal judgments. When we accommodate the schisms of alienation we live by the short-sighted self-interest of institutional religion. Authentic religion and personal conscience do not abide alienation .

Scandalizing the Innocents

Fundamentally linked to "Old School" (Tridentine) Catholicism is the deep-rooted traumatizing of personal consciousness, a wound that if not consciously aware is nevertheless carved into the impressionable psyche of the subconscious. Vatican II appropriately still unsettles people, as well it should. The scandalizing of innocents (breach of trust) is about as bad as sin gets.

More than ten years before Vatican II I came to understand how innocents are victims of breached faith (the "Religious Paralysis Syndrome," RPS, which is not recognized by the hierarchy even now). Vatican II came to the commonsense recognition that EVOLUTION IS AND HAS BEEN HAPPENING. So, WHEN WILL THE CHURCH BE NOT AFRAID to say the word "evolution," admit the fact of it, and teach it?

I understand that Tridentine theology (scholastic philosophy — "primary" male-"secondary" female) may be no problem in some people's mind. It is however, I think, problematic for everyone when kids are indoctrinated in a culture of guilt and fear from their tenderest years, on premises of the Adam-and-Eve rib story and before they have the intellectual maturity to deal with such a weighty and consequential presumption — and boys are immediately transitioned from eighth grade into the seminary at thirteen years of age, as I and many others did before and after me.

In the beginning of his journey to the priesthood, the young man starts out with a fraudulent sense of human sexuality that is without scientific credibility — and childhood indoctrination is confirmed in the seminary, his trauma is deepened and he is further disabled to question or doubt his prejudiced sexual upbringing.

I came to my crisis of conscience at the end of Philosophy, age 23. I stayed on in the Seminary one more year as recommended by Father John Musinsky, SVD, and I'm glad I did because during First Year Theology he and I both came to understand better where I come from. When I left the Seminary he did me the courtesy of driving me to the L-Station.

Until church opens to evolution and admits evolution's relevance to theology and ecclesiology, church cannot reasonably expect people not to challenge it. It is wrongheaded to fixate minds of the faithful in the medieval inauthenticity of Trent/ Vatican I, and more specifically, it is an inexcusable scandal that violates innocence. There is no returning to the Tridentine past. It is long overdue to stop the repetitious culture of scandal.

No Solution but Compassion

There is no solution to life's conundrum except, compassion for all, and fidelity to Personal Truth. Graced nature is a daily lesson of faithful living.

The direction of evolution is toward greater complexity; and with increased complexity, more challenge, more misunderstanding and occasion for violence, but also opportunity for continuing redemption. Admittedly, it isn't easy to disagree without being disagreeable; but fidelity to personal truth, to Earth's intelligence, requires openness to the truth in other, for it is by openness that we become rooted and grow in Godlikeness.

Culturally we tend toward polarization and seeing "truth" in unambiguous, clear-cut, black-and-white terms. The reality is that truth comes to us in shades of light and darkness. For example, the truth about violence is that it is a "cultural thing" and we give in to it out of habit. On reflection we must admit that non-violence is also an option of culture, more in the interest of all than violence. Dispositions of mind are radically changeable because the cortical brain is dialogically open to right reason. Adaptability of reason is a matter of conscious disposition and intentional motivation.

Eucharist is a consciousness that pursues right order in the interest of self and other. Such pursuit serves immediate interest and disposes toward habits of serving the mutual interests of self and other on into the future. Commonsense informs consciousness that persistence in authentic behavior, in the moment, can, by determination of will and consistence of habit, keep one on the right course now and in the future.

Jesus says, "As I have done, you also should do." The example of Jesus is Eucharist. In celebrating the Mass we remember who Jesus is, what Jesus did, and what we in real life are to become, to be, i.e., Eucharist to one another.

COMPASSION — the Symbiotic Virtue

Compassion is the healing balm of a hurting world, the gracious way of living together mindfully and purposely. What is the difference between symbiosis and Eucharist? Symbiosis has from life's beginnings been the evolving mechanism of chemical/ biological interactivity — prior to self-reflective consciousness. Eucharist is intentional compassion, the focus of self-reflective consciousness on personal/ social wellbeing. Eucharist is "symbiosis on purpose," the

Godlike virtue of compassionate mutuality, the intentional virtue of healing.

And what does "compassionate" mean? passion means "suffering," and "com" means with; so, compassion means suffering with. Compassion is about shared hurting, suffering one another's pain. We can only be compassionate if we appreciate the necessity of suffering together. Real compassion requires us to intend no harm to others, and that means to do what we can to mitigate hurt, to eliminate causes to the extent we can, and above all to do no willful harm. We are enabled to live compassionately by trustful communication, informed consciousness and committed conscience.

Compassion isn't experienced in isolation; alienation is a bar to compassion. A church that alienates is non-Eucharistic. Compassion shares knowledge, insights and understanding — the way of coming to compassionate, Eucharistic living. Wisdom and health are mutual benefits of compassionate living.

WORD UNLIMITED seeks to tap in to the well of Eucharistic consciousness, the waters of healing. Compassion, dialog, are "confessional" virtues, virtues that lead to forgiveness and purposes of amendment that heal and mitigate causes of hurt. Faith, hope and love are graces of communication, consciousness and conscience, the virtues and means of Eucharistic Altruism, intentional symbiosis.

JUSTIFIED BY GOD

Being "True to Faith" is not the same as submitting to the imposition of the faith-expectations of others on one's faith, one's truth. When one lives by the habit of holding faith accountable to truth, and truth accountable to reason, one lives by the Law of Personal Conscience.

No law is so compelling, so reassuring and fearless, as the Law of Conscience that holds true to faith. It's the integrity of faith's certitude that sets one free and makes one fearless in the face of fideistic violence. No pope, no monarch, no despot has the power to destroy the confidence and peace of mind that comes to the person who is True to Faith, TRUE TO PERSONAL CONSCIENCE. The Truth will hold you free, and the Truth is: men are not "primary" and women are not "secondary." This truth can set The Church free and liberate women and nature from alienation and exploitation.

Institutional Catholicism has not yet separated itself from the "dogma" of alienation and exploitation; its fixation in acceptance of the ancient Creation Mythology calls for urgent witness to Nature and the integrity of the Human Person, FEMALE-MALE CHARACTERIZED — in God's Image.

Nature is perishing, and we are perishing with Her.

http://www.gather.com/viewArticle.action?articleId=2814749793 52523

OIL vs. WATER, the PETRINE vs. the MARIAN

The crisis of global energy is a metaphor for the crisis of religious relevance. The subordination of value, of right order, of oil over water, is tantamount to the subordination of female priesthood to male and the reversal of the "Naturalis Sacramentum Ordinis."

The reversal of this order by Roman Catholic culture is the triumph of ignorance over faith and arrogance over reason. Distrust and violence feed off each other as trust (faith) and humility (reason) feed off each other. Where oil presumes ordination over water, distrust and violence prevail over faith and reason.

The alienation of women from ordination in church culture effectively alienates people from each other and human culture from respect for nature, from the COSMIC ORDINATION of nature. The Order of Nature depends from/ on cosmic resonances in the order of evolution, biology and theology; except for evolution, there is no life; except for life, there is no conscious biology; and except for rightly informed consciousness there is no authentic theology, no cultural conscience, no compassion. When theology denies evolution, it denies its own causality. Absent respect for the Sacrament of Natural Order, communication fails faith, consciousness fails hope, and conscience fails love.

The frustration of faith, hope and love is the antithesis to Trinitarian Harmony, the realm of the anti-Christ, the frustration of divine co-ordination, natural necessity and spiritual sanity. The Dark Ages hold power over light in the culture of female/ male alienation, in the culture of the "Petrine" over the "Marian," of "oil" over "water." This is the crisis of Roman Catholicism, the global crisis of nature; both must be corrected together or neither will be corrected.

Neither Superior nor Inferior

Humankind is a family of equals before God. The arrogation of male superiority over women, and claim of divine favor, is an obvious cultural deception of intentional dominion and overreach that cannot stand. The reverse arrogation of women over man is also not valid in light of the Divine/ human hypostasis. The pride of such arrogation defeats grace in the Naturalis Sacramentum Ordinis.

Comparisons are odious, and so it is unseemly for females to self-arrogate, even though they are ontologically prior to males and could with greater justification claim hierarchical superiority over males. Before God, there is no favoritism of person. All of humankind is of a kind, and the whole of the cosmos is of a piece. In God there is neither female nor male; the distinction of the human person is equality before God.

In the disposition of the Naturalis Sacramentum Ordinis, it is right and proper for every person to enter with common purpose into the Universal Sacrament of Eucharist, and grow, experience conversion, and witness by ritual the Sacred Remembrance in appropriate manner as befits equality and identity in Universal Eucharist.

Males have alienated females from their rightful role of equivalency in Church. It is for women, as life-bearers of the Person of Jesus to continue in perpetual birthing the nurturing of the Cosmic Christ. Children in the Person of Christ are "persons of Second Coming." None enters the kingdom of God except as a child, and except with the Eucharistic Fiat of woman.

The Person of Christ is in the person of Mary as the person of Mary is in the Person of Christ. And so it is in the Cosmic Order of the Naturalis Sacramentum Ordinis. The interpersonal identity of female/ male is in every person as in the Persona Christi. By common origin in water (Baptism), the Hypostasis of the Divine/ human is destined in ever-perfecting consciousness by way of Eucharistic Altruism, and by way of the resurrection of consciousness from death to birth, from birth to death.

In the resurrection and ascendance of Eucharistic Altruism, personal identity and mutuality of the Divine and human make holy with grace the Naturalis Sacramentum Ordinis. In Godlikeness, female and male persons are equal also in their priestly call to service in Church.

Global Corporate Capitalism

Global Corporate Capitalism has evolved from colonialism, colonialism from the feudalism of European (Roman imperial) Kingdom States; what these cultural forms retain in common is top-down dominion in which nature and people are dominated by the profit interests of a religious/ political elite, now the Western corporate capitalists and the money market engineers — Stock Exchanges. The rift between the rich and the poor widens instead of contracts, creating an ever larger population of destitute people— not a pretty picture, and certainly not a sustainable one, but a recipe for violence and perpetual class (political/religious) wars. The Commons have been privatized, prostituted.

Indigenous people and bioregional resources are capitalized to conform to Western models of corporate control and exploitation, e.g., energy intensive agriculture and the chemical domination of biological systems. Energy-intensive agriculture is new and not sustainable because of its intense mono-culturing (species destruction) and gene-manipulation.

Nature has always provided for people by means of bioregional resources, including solar energy. These means (The Commons) are sustainably preserved in the bioregional context of flora and fauna, and under necessities of mutuality, complementarity and subsidiarity. Energy intense, heavy equipment farming is biologically ruthless and unsustainable.

The world-wide importation of energy-intensive agriculture destroys bioregional web-life, corrupts the social order of people, trashes the environment and drives species to extinction. Technologies need to function with respect for and in context with bioregional flora and fauna.

Corporate capitalism needs to convert to "communal capitalism" in which the whole community is invested — in this way the bioregion capitalizes on its unique vitality, both, that of the people and the diversity of localities.

Dead-End Exclusivity

Sustainability is all about adaptability — that is nature's lesson of evolution and the cultural lesson of history. It is in the nature of wave/ particle dynamics to be open-ended, that is, to be adaptable to change and open to accommodate. Exclusivity is imprisonment, is the building of impermeable walls that are closed to change and adaptability; the arrogant assumption that no more change is needed flies in the face of life-experience. Trust in God and nature is open to potentials of natural conditions.

Closed systems die by the dogma of their self-sufficiency — including patent-exclusive technologies that alter and control the trajectory of genetic evolution. Nature knows how to remain open-ended, corporate technology does not for it seeks to eliminate competition. Nowhere in nature is there evidence that life is not adaptable to change. Species that can't adapt become extinct. Sometimes the demands for change put on species are too radical and too sudden, so that despite themselves they are driven to extinction. It's happening now. Industrial waste, pollution, excessive exploitation and genetic modifications are putting radical demands on web-life beyond its ability to adapt and accommodate.

Religious dogma, the rationale of closed thinking, is a model that justifies all the wrong things humans are doing to nature and themselves; by its blind dogma, cultures are condemning themselves to sure death just as surely as they are causing the unprecedented extinction of species.

Ignorance, arrogance and obsession are the trinitarian antithesis, the vices of closed dogma and dominion culture. Open trinitarian culture, enabled to change and adapt by reason of its open dynamic of communication, consciousness and conscience, has an open future, for it engages the Godlike rationale required to overcome the dead-end destruction of ultimate narcissism. Church dogmatism and corporate consumerism root in closed-minded narcissism, whose idolatrous, male-presumed self-sufficiency is the blight of reason and faith.

Evolution, symbiosis and Eucharistic Altruism embody the Trinitarian dynamism that keeps cultures open to survival, adaptability and change. Grace supposes nature as faith supposes reason; authentic culture supposes authentic religion in which FAITH HOLDS REASON ACCOUNTABLE AND REASON HOLDS FAITH ACCOUNTABLE.

People, we are Church, we are government. Let's learn to live by Eucharistic openness and accommodate by way of cultural authenticity.

Thesis and Anti-Thesis of Theistic Evolution

The Paramount Question for Global Christianity is: "What is the theological/ ecclesial future for Global Culture?" The trajectory of ascendant consciousness (evolution) is from symbiotic instinct (natural necessity-determination) to the intuitional mindedness (purpose) of Christic Altruism and the mindfulness of self-transformation into Other.

Religiously, this trajectory is driven by the "withinness" of the Sacrament of Natural Order, which derives from the conscious reality of female (Marian) priority over the male-dominant (Petrine.) The authenticity of church structure is challenged by the theology of the primacy of "the Marian over the Petrine," and so are structures of corporate consumerism. The frustration of religion/ civility up to now is the frustration of antithetical culture, i.e., of the male-dominant overreach of people and nature.

The Trinitarian Thesis underlying Marian (feminine) priority is the open vision of God as WORD-LIGHT-LOVE, as opposed to the male-antithetical vision fixated in ignorance, arrogance and obsession — artifices of the supposed priority of the Petrine (masculinity) over the Marian (femininity).

Accountable Faith — Accountable Reason

Evolution's intuitional self-reflection has lifted consciousness above a morbid attitude toward death to a hopeful sense of resurrection. The challenge of the Cosmic Christic Mission is to redeem nature from the violence of exploitation and restore bioregional webs to the open potentials of diverse life, the Common Ground of human sustainability. The challenge specifically, is to motivate the sustainable grace of Eucharistic Altruism so as to rescue diverse life from the mindless exploitation of cultural dominion and theological alienation. Called for is the conscious embrace of difference and the integration of differences for the worthy purposes they serve, instead of out-of-hand rejection of the unfamiliar, the "other."

We are called to reciprocate in kind what we receive from nature. Our self-reflective consciousness is ultimately the gift of instinctive symbiosis; however, instinct is violence-driven in self-interest. The use of violence by the dominant species (humankind) puts all other species at risk unless the dominant species is aware of its self-destructive power, and avoids overreach. The life and teaching of Jesus, the Cosmic Christ, exposes the antithesis of cultural dominion and its violent, unsustainable overreach of people and nature, and gives the sustainable alternative of Eucharistic Altruism.

What distinguishes Eucharist from symbiosis is that it is purpose-driven (soft-wired) and not instinct-driven (hard-wired.) Christic Consciousness focuses self-reflection on the Godlike virtue of conscionable choosing whose interest is in other as in self. The hermeneutic (reflective interpretation) of symbiotic history leads to the logic and necessity of Eucharistic Altruism, intentional avoidance of violence toward other, and the willingness of self to secure other in the witting giving of self to other. Nature models the way of mindfulness in symbiotic interests, that is, in the necessary transformation of self from other and into other. Faith in the purposes of Godlikeness compels the altruism of Eucharist. Reason is accountable to Faith, even as Faith is accountable to Reason. "Faith supposes reason as Grace supposes nature." [John Courtney Murray, SJ, — The Second Vatican Council]

When Prejudice becomes Dogma

BAD THINGS HAPPEN when prejudice becomes dogma; for example, prejudice-made-dogma is behind the alienation of women from church and of humankind from symbiotic fidelity. When we get nature wrong, we get religion wrong.

Persuasions and prejudices — we all have them, for better and for worse — but when a persuasion becomes a prejudice, and a prejudice becomes a fixed belief, we begin an inner entanglement that shows itself in ways hurtful to ourselves and others. Earth, humankind and web-life suffer the same tragedy at the hands of the prejudice of male thinking that arrogantly elevates males above and apart from real co-dependency within nature, humankind and web-life.

The arrogation of prejudice-made-dogma happens all too easily for it fits the convenience of male politics to exploit nature and others in self-advantage. Once a power structure puts its preferred dogma in place, there is no telling the ultimate consequences. Given the degraded condition of nature, the oppression of women, and the conflicted relationship of world religions/ people, it's time to think seriously about what is in common behind these sorry circumstances.

Persuasions are tendencies of thinking in-process of development. As we acquire knowledge, our persuasions may be reinforced, tweaked a little or a lot, or totally discarded. If we prematurely give a partially informed persuasion the standing of prejudice, we become judgmental and misguided, thereby putting ourselves in the obnoxious position of being overbearing and without credibility. Prejudice-made-dogma has become the religion of patriarchal dominion.

The children of Abraham, Judaic, Christian and Islamic, are unaccommodating in the way they cling to their preferred versions of divine "male-chosenism." The religious culture of dogmatic arrogance shows little prospect of reconciliation. The truthfulness of authentic judgment and relationship is what authentic religion and purposeful humanity are about.

Perhaps reconciliation can happen if we step back and admit our inheritance of original conflicts rooted in sibling animosities. It is in the nature of truth-seeking-consciousness to be open to new learning and to accommodate persuasions without prejudice to self and other. Misinformed presumptions (persuasions-made-dogma) are not only undoing us socially/ culturally, but are undoing the Symbiotic Commons of nature.

Openness to evolution can help us debunk the arrogant religious culture of too-soon jumping from persuasion to dogma. "If we surrender to Earth intelligence we could become rooted, like trees. Instead we entangle ourselves in knots of our own making and struggle, alone and confused." (Rilke, "A Year with Rilke")

Why does the Vatican

… and Christianity perpetuate the root abuse of women that enables other forms of sexual abuse, namely, that women are denied equal respect and authority with men for no reason other than that they are females; males hold women in inferior standing on presumption that women are originally "secondary," inferior to males, and are ontologically derived in person (Eve) from the male (Adam) person? Evolution history exposes the wrongness of this absurd presumption.

Until the Vatican acknowledges this fundamentally flawed presumption, flawed scientifically and intuitionally, Roman Catholicism will never get to the bottom of the problem of other manifestations of sexual abuse. Habituated dominion and overreach blind males to the fact of their misogyny and instinct to dominate and exploit sex in self-interest. This "article of faith" is in fact an "article of fideism" that traumatizes faith. The People cannot abide this insanity.

The message of patriarchal pomposity and dominion is that it is beholden to instinctual aggression and the fraud of presumptive male-superiority; this male instinctive arrogance alienates female intuition and sensitivity (the trust basis of faith) from essential roles of witnessing communal compassion and the rightful and needed defense of children against male abuse, sexual and cultural. Jesus is revolutionary precisely because He let the intuitional inheritance He received from His mom dominate His life and Gospel.

GREEN RELIGION: the Sign and Grace of Trinity

Triatomic processing in Nature is "Green Sacrament." Water (H-O-H) and carbon-dioxide (O-C-O) are disassembled and reassembled by light (photon) in the green chlorophyll molecule. The wave/ particle efficiency of molecular energy (the grace of light) is signified in Green Nature. The medium of transformational dialogue is infrared light; the greenness of Nature announces the Trinitarian Processing of TRIMORPHIC RESONANCE.

The "three-ness" of Nature's Green is the God-Grace of Trimorphic Resonance. Nature's Green Grace is preconditioned in evolution's Wisdom and Age. WISDOM-AGE-GRACE, like FAITH-HOPE-LOVE, like COMMUNICATION-CONSCIOUSNESS-CONSCIENCE, like WORD-LIGHT-LOVE are each the precondition of the other.

WORD is the precondition of Communication, as LIGHT is the precondition of Consciousness, as LOVE is the precondition of Conscience. COMMUNICATION is the precondition of Faith, as CONSCIOUSNESS is the precondition of Hope, as CONSCIENCE is the precondition of Love. FAITH is the precondition of Wisdom, as HOPE is the precondition of Age, as Love is the precondition of Grace. All the above is reciprocally true when the correlations are put in reverse order — for the Cosmos originates in Singularity, and all within the Cosmos relates commonly in energy/ matter, in soul/ substance. As Isaiah says, "All flesh is grass."

In the Trinitarian processing of resonances, evolution proceeds in codependent mutuality, complementarity and subsidiarity. Cosmic waves/ particles operate in all things in effecting Trinitarian outcomes. WORD-LIGHT-LOVE are coefficient resources of purposeful life, what are: GREEN RELIGION, EVOLUTION THEOLOGY, and EUCHARISTIC SACRAMENT.

INTELLIGENCE -Gathering and –Using

Intelligence gathering is a conscious process of information collecting. It is uniquely human in that the gathering of information is a reasoned process of communication and consciousness intended for purposes of understanding and putting to use information/ experiences that work in beneficial ways. Using intelligence for purposes of personal/ social wellbeing is the "wise" thing to do. The person who is judicious in decisions and purposeful in actions is considered a person of wisdom.

Because every action has consequences, it makes sense to mindfully anticipate consequences before taking actions. Unintended consequences occur even with the most carefully reasoned plans. The talent for making intellectual judgments is mostly an acquired virtue. It is a talent (grace) that has been long in the process of evolving. Throughout most of evolution, trial-and-error was the mode of learning. Intelligence is a learning that originated in and came out of the school of hard-knocks. Evolved intelligence has the advantage of a long history of acquired experience which is a library of information (cumulative intuitional wisdom) accessible to inform judgments in the face of new experience.

In the present time, we are heir to a catastrophic heap of experiential disasters that require remedial action to break the chain of bad actions and consequences pulling humankind toward disaster. As elders, we owe our children more than leaving them to deal with our complicit history of mindlessness toward nature and moral relationships.

The right and proper use of intelligence is not only the intelligent thing to do, it is the moral thing to do, for, the hard-knocks way of doing relationships is avoidable to a certain extent in the face of knowledge that is available to avoid repeat experiences of hurt. The intelligent use of communication and consciousness compels us to take the next step and recognize the moral obligation of acting conscionably, reasonably, with knowledge of consequences.

The intelligent use of information supposes morality and common sense, for morality and rationality have in common the wellbeing of the individual person, the community, and the natural order of diverse life from which and upon which all depend. Becoming "Godlike" is the process of owning intelligence (wisdom) and applying it judiciously. Evolution Theology is an intelligence process of gathering and using intelligence against unanticipated circumstances. It is a medium of engaging information gathering and using. Join the process at

http://godtalkonline.blogspot.com/2011/08/evolution-theology. html .

The Gospel of Altruism

The WORD of Gospel has at heart the purifying power of altruism. True Heart kindles altruistic love, compassion, the fervor that compels the "Priesthood of Service." God talk is the language of altruism, the fire of Eucharist.

Altruistic love, the fervor of true heart, seriously intends other-concern. "Heralds of the Gospel" are driven by true heart. It is the love of other that burns off the dross of ego-fixation. Love that is altruistic isn't possible unless mindfulness is keen in knowing the corruptive consequences of self-adulation. Other-concern is the Godlike virtue of compassion that identifies God in other. If God is Other and we chose ego over Other, what kind of sin is that? It is the sin of idolatry. To honor self over Other is idolatry.

Eucharistic Altruism is Godlike in compassion for it puts service to other on a par with divine service. The Priesthood of Service to Other is a Cosmic anointing, an anointing confirmed in the rite of baptism and open to all God's People.

WORD Unlimited is LIGHT Unlimited, LOVE Unlimited — ICONIC TRINITY

DIVINICOM is Divinity Communication — Altruistic WORD

DIVINICON is Divinity Consciousness — Altruistic LIGHT

DIVINICOR is Divinity Conscience — Altruistic LOVE

If we don't get Nature right, we don't get God right.

http://www.ncronline.org/news/justice/after-debt-ceiling-crisis-real-work-us-social-policy-lies-ahead#comment-247813

http://www.authorhouse.com/Bookstore/BookSearchResults.aspx?Search=Green%20Religion

http://www.gather.com/viewArticle.action?articleId=281474979838542

The Deadly Social Sins

Gandhi

Politics without Principle

Wealth without Work

Commerce without Morality

Pleasure without Conscience

Education without Character

Science without Humanity

Worship without Sacrifice

Seven Deadly Social Sins

Courtesy of SOJOURNERS Magazine

The cult of incivility is rooted in three deadly social sins which directly defeat the civil virtues of faith, hope and love. These sins devastate personal and communal life; they fly directly in the face of Christian Trinity and must, therefore, be considered as blasphemy by Christians. These sins can be expressed in the manner of the seven deadly social sins listed by Mohandas K. Gandhi. They are: words without work, procreation without provision, and civitas without civilitas.

Words without Work: The fraud of word-only spirituality is that it justifies itself without accountability for its connection to the working of natural necessity. God's Word is self-bound in natural Work. True Sacrament embodies in work its consciousness of word, unlike word-only rite and ritual. True word raises conscious-ness by its efficiency in doing in secular (material) reality what it says. The reliable embodiment of word is the fact-basis of faith; empty words are fruitless for they lack the faith-inspiration of work's embodiment. The pretense of words at odds with work puts God to the test and trashes Natural Order.

Procreation without Provision: Hope is consciously inspired in the experience of Nature's reliable provisioning of life. Hope is defeated when the providence of life is desecrated. Excessive human numbers and appetites are viciously wasting network life. True worship of God holds Providence sacred and sustains the largesse of network life for future generations. Where humans settle, history shows a mindless absence of foresight and the mindless waste of life. The conscienceless destruction of natural providence is a hope-destroying act that unmasks the lie of pretentious belief in God's Providence — a fearsome mockery of God.

Civitas without Civilitas: The collective breaches of faith and hope ultimately work their devastation on love. Without love for one another people obsess in egoism and neglect confessional living that acknowledges the debt responsibility of bearing one another's burdens and sharing life's gifts. Individual life and its giftedness is a gratuity of previous life that belongs also to future generations. The violation of communal love is a violation of conscience. Without civility, without lived faith/ hope/ love, there can be no City of God, no harmonious community. The defeat of love is the ultimate sin against God who is Love.

The Purpose of Schools: Educate or Indoctrinate?

ROMAN Catholicism (and Christian denominations, to a lesser extent) is a cultic religion, tightly managed by an elite male hierarchy which sees its role in holding to a self-presumed, infallible superiority; their infallibility control extends over women, nature and property. Their prideful presumption subdues all to status of commodities, chattel. Their mode of control is strict and early indoctrination, and the symbolism of the cross and the sword to instill permanent imprints of guilt and fear. Political control of mind and body is imposed in symbol and fact.

The wisdom of Evolution Theology exposes the secrets of dominion culture, of the male hierarchical cult. As long as education is structured to indoctrinate the strategies of guilt and fear, cultic male hierarchy succeeds in control purposes. Indoctrination intends control; education intends self-authentication.

If male cultic strategies are challenged by Evolution Theology, education begins to see its objective in brighter light — not to prop up dominion culture but to free people and nature from gratuitous exploitation. The indoctrination of children early in guilt and fear is oppressive, offensive, unjust and contrary to the Good News Gospel. Divinity Consciousness is compassionate, not oppressive — as Jesus informs, "my yoke is easy and the burden light."

CHURCH — Eucharistic, or "Roman?"

Class-structured religion, as in patriarchal theology, is on its face a religion that divides for cultic purposes. People are stratified in classes for arbitrary reasons, birth, education, wealth, etc., for self and institutional purposes. People are not presumed to be equal in all regards as a mother might consider her children.

Evolution Theology, as the intentional theology of life, sees essential equality as the presumptive relationship of individual life derived from same origins. The relationship of equality is of reciprocal dependency, egalitarian co-dependency, not class-stratified to meter out advantage and disadvantage.

The transformational character of cosmic evolution is the reality of Eucharistic necessity, of all coming from "other" and destined to return to "other." The consciousness of Eucharistic necessity is the root consciousness of Christic Altruism, for it is cosmic necessity that holds in common the energy/ substance correlations of transformation.

The Church of Sacrament is the Church of Remembrance, the Church of Eucharistic Altruism. Eucharistic mindfulness, with or without ritual, is the necessity of intentional Eucharist, intentional community, what is the "Eucharistic Catholic Church." Sacrament, Eucharist, REALITY, matter more than theatre. Reality is Eucharist, mindful openness to reality is mindful Eucharist — Eucharistic Altruism. The Church of the Future is "Eucharistic," not "Roman" but catholic.

Why is Jesus' father Joseph all but lost to history while his Mother Mary has a compelling presence? Does this say something about the inauthenticity of present day patriarchal culture? The mother-son relationship is the Christic sign of compassion, while the father-son relationship is a sign of contradiction, competition, one-up-man-ship, and dominion-quest.

The EUCHARISTIC CATHOLIC CHURCH eschews the principle and outcome of the male presumptive cult in favor of mother-child compassionate culture.

The Pope's "Army," alive and ... well?

If you thought the Wars of Crusades against Islam had been put to rest, consider this. The Pope's Army, the Knights Templar is alive and active in personal service to popes. Pope Benedict XVI has just appointed a new supreme commander to oversee the business of the Knights Templar Army.

The Knights Equestrian Order of the Holy Sepulcher of Jerusalem is based in Rome. Its new Pro-Grand Master is Archbishop Edwin O'Brien of Baltimore. The Order is a "chivalric organization dedicated" to promote and defend the Latin Patriarch. The Patriarchy dates back to the First Crusade that "liberated Jerusalem."

In response to the appointment that takes him to Rome, the Archbishop said, "It is with a heavy heart that I will carry out the will of God and the pope in preserving the faith in the Holy Land."

[The WITNESS, Dubuque Iowa Archdiocesan Weekly, 9/4/2011, pg. 14]

The Legacy of Vatican II

Revelation is the evolutionary dynamic of Church. How do Revelation and Church relate? They relate as unity and continuity. In one Word, they are EUCHARIST, we are Eucharist. In the book "Revelation and the Church, Vatican II in the Twenty-First Century," Edited by Raymond A. Lucker and William C. McDonough, © 2003, Orbis Books, Maryknoll, New York 10545, pg. 228ff, the questions are raised: which comes first, Revelation or Church? Does it matter?

Are Revelation and Church coincident in the identification of one with the other? Bishop Raymond A. Lucker makes us rethink Revelation and Church in light of the Second Vatican Council. Revelation and Church present the same moral mandate, to be and to live Eucharist. This is the legacy of Vatican II.

Church and Revelation have the same two faces, one as "gift," and one as "task." Gift and task give order to personal, social living. In Bishop Lucker's words, gift and task are about "how to be a good church, how to be a renewed church, and how to touch the hearts of the people." One who seeks personal renewal is engaged in the task and gift of Church renewal. It is in the seeker's pursuit of renewal (task) that the gift of Revelation, Church, is experienced. "What shall I return to the Lord for all his bounty to me? ...I will pay my vows to the Lord in the presence of his people." (Psalm 1:16, 12-15)

Life's task is ultimately fulfilled in the renewal of gift. We are life's task, we are life's gift, we are revelation, and we are church. Life well-lived is aware of task, of gift, and seeks fulfillment that renews, generation upon generation. "Church ...insists that whatever we claim to know of God either leads toward life shared with others or it is a deception... Revelation ...insists that whatever order we have established is provisional — part of a final, full order hidden in God."

Vatican II illumines the truth that "the earthly church and the church endowed with heavenly riches are not to be thought of as two realms. On the contrary, they form one complex reality comprising a human and a divine element." (Lumen Gentium, 8)

We deceive ourselves when we separate church-invisible from church-visible. We, God's people are church-visible in the present time and not to be disjoined from church-past and church-future. In task and gift, by fidelity to faith, hope and love, we are Church and Revelation.

The Electrical/ Chemical Person

Self-reflective consciousness calls all to celebrate the electrical ambiguity of chemistry.

The priesthood of Eucharistic working, like DNA, intends the middle way of symbiotic reconciliation. It takes femininity and masculinity together to nullify the pathogenic alienation of lethal egoism.

People! Celebrate the ambiguity of electricity! Men! Celebrate the feminine side of your humanity! Women! Celebrate the masculine side of your humanity! Let the electricity of chemistry work the magic of nature and reconcile the polarities of faith and reason!

IV. WISDOM —
the Grace of Intelligence

The Harmonic Grid of Evolving Complexity

[Implicated Patterns of Trimorphic Resonance]

COSMOLOGY	PHILOSOPHY	THEOLOGY
Chaos	Structure	Synchrony
Divergence	Convergence	Emergence
Dissonance	Consonance	Attenuation
Communication	Consciousness	Conscience
Dialogue	Discernment	Decision
Identity	Otherness	Altruism
Instinct	Intuition	Intelligence
Uncertainty	Consensus	Purpose
Reason	Enlightenment	Redemption
Wisdom	Age	Grace
Mutuality	Complementarity	Subsidiarity
Birth	Growth	Death
Baptism	Confirmation	Eucharist
Faith	Hope	Love
Politics	Religion	Government
Past	Present	Future

Openness to Word, Worldview, Wisdom

Mostly, the problem people have with my writing is more about concepts than language, namely, unfamiliarity with Evolution Theology, the theology of change. Christianity and all religions in general remain prisoners to the concepts and language of the Static-Centrist Worldview, and uninformed in the concepts and language of the Evolutionary Worldview. Once consciousness adjusts to world-view change, Word Unlimited becomes more transparent, more refreshing.

Time to be SHAMELESSLY HONEST

Too long, dishonesty prevails globally in religious/ political cultures. The calamity of cultural lies and maladjustment now contribute to interpersonal violence, the doing-in of nature's ecological economics, and putting at risk the very survival of global humanity. Fixations in misinformation compound cultural misdirection.

Common embryonic rudiments determine the sexual character of both females and males. The differentiation of female/ male sexuality in the individual embryo occurs with the differentiation of originally indistinguishable sex buds. The biological saying "ontogeny recapitulates phylogeny" states the principle that individual embryonic development is an iteration of the evolutionary history of the phylum.

In the determination of sexual differentiation there is no priority, no superiority or inferiority. Females and males both have nipples; males don't have a uterus, but in rudimentary origin the prostate is the equivalent; females don't have a penis, but the clitoris is equivalent in its rudimentary origin; males don't have ovaries, but testicles are equivalent in rudimentary origin. In every physical and psychological aspect, females and males are essentially correlated.

Humankind needs Maternal Wisdom now more than ever; the

Wisdom of the Divine Feminine can lead the way from the culture of deception and death to the authentic nurture of Graced Nature.

The complicit theology underlying the politics of corporate consumerism is unconscionable and unsustainable. The Static-Centrist Worldview continues to promote these self-serving deceits, which will remain until religion and culture are open to the redemptive potentials of evolutionary transformation and the ascendant consciousness of Divinity.

There is a kind of church we can well do without, i.e., the "church-ignorant, church-arrogant, church-obsessive;" it is for people to be the People Church of faith, hope and love, open and compassionate — Eucharistic.

In the "becoming of being," every person is a "herald of Eucharist," of good news understanding life's purpose and trajectory. In the mindfulness of Sacred Remembrance, Eucharistic sensitivity holds life's trajectory on true course.

Evolution Theology

http://godtalkonline.blogspot.com/2011/08/evolution-theology.html

(ET) Item 1: Website Announcement

From our own experience we know that personal intelligence evolves. This is applies to every aspect of consciousness, including theological consciousness. Growing up coached by institutional religion, it is likely that we have a sense that theological consciousness is owned by and passed on by the church of our birth. The conflicts of institutional religions, all of whom claim truth, cause us to pause and consider who owns religion, truth.

Conversations here of personal religion are opportunities to share with others your personal sense of religious truth and to enlarge your faith inheritance from birth. For discussion topics you are invited to visit these websites:

www.evolution101.org
www.secondenlightenment.org
www.divinicom.com
www.acolyte.gather.com
www.wordunlimited.com

ET Item 2: Categories of Closed Thinking

Though the Cosmos unfolds in sustainable patterns, it is not locked in fixed categories — rather it is in constant transformation at the level of deep wave/ particle dynamics.

Only the small-mindedness of human misinformation fixes itself in categories of closed thinking — but even these are destined to collapse over time in the determined evolution of self-reflective consciousness.

Institutional religions invest in fixed categories and lose credibility when the deceits of fixations are exposed. Age is no handicap to newness, on the contrary, age is the condition of newness, of death, birth, redemption, resurrection — the way of Evolution Theology (ET).

The schism of cleaving the material from the spiritual, the body from soul, is irrational, counter-intuitive and self-destructive. The presumption that soul and body are distinct and separate is a fixated category of misinformed thinking. The self-identity of the human person is mangled by the ill-begotten schism of soul/ body. The substance/ energy of the Cosmos is the continuity reality of symbiotic evolution.

Spiritual arrogance toward material nature enables the cultural sin of corporate exploitation of nature and environmental wasting. Ecological wasting is at the root of presently occurring economic collapses and global indebtedness. If we abuse the energy/ substance of nature, we abuse ourselves. We can stop abusing ourselves by stopping our abuse of nature. Religions need redemption and so do cultures and nature.

ET Item 3: Sexuality and Theology

Sexuality is the self-reproductive nature of life. Evolution Theology is about relational life, about female/ male equivalency in Divinity. Evolution is about the genetics of Earth-life and so is theological/ religious consciousness. Sexuality is the root relationship of life and consciousness.

Arguably, sexual abuse is the critical issue of nature and religion. What is sexual abuse? A woman's answer is probably very different from a man's. Men are likely to qualify (justify) their answer in the Garden of Eden Mandate, "increase and multiply." Women, on the other hand, might be more nuanced in their answer and see the Second Mandate as equally and necessarily applicable.

The Second Mandate forbids the consumption of the vitality (fruit) of the Middle Tree. The "Tree in the Middle of the Garden" is collectively life's diverse webs sustaining interdependent nature. Web-life vitality is a condition of human existence; humankind cannot successfully increase and multiply except for life's eco-codependent webs. The excess "success" of one species — humankind — is destroying sustainable web-life. The specter of African mothers and children walking miles and miles through lifeless terrains is a warning to global humanity, and a sign of excess humankind destroying self and nature. Male hierarchical put-down of females in religious culture is of-a-piece with abusive consumer exploitation of nature.

Evolution Theology brings to the surface of religious/ cultural consciousness the critical issue of the time, what is sexual abuse, prostitution; the many faces of waste root in the religious/ political justification of male priority/ superiority.

ET Item 4: From Mytheology to Eartheology

And, whence comes divinity consciousness, from myth or from earth? Myth is an unfolding story of human imagination; conscious Earth-life is the source of myth and divinity consciousness. But Old Testament myth has been made dogma by closed theological thinking; and, evolution is denied by cultures excluding it from theological consideration.

Don't get me wrong. I'm not saying that mythology has no theological truth in it, only that theology should remain open to Earth-insights. Abrahamic religions and Western cultures root in Old Testament mythology/ theology. Literal mytheology is fantasy theology. Belief in God is no myth, but is the consensus consciousness of times immemorial, even though regional histories and experience construe their own myths.

Cultural experience knows that writers use different techniques of writing for specific reasons, e.g., poetry, history, biography, mythologies, novels, etc. Personal interests and political circumstances condition a writer's thinking and perspective. These human factors apply also in sacred writings of all times.

Credit post-Reformation Scripture scholars (other than Roman Catholic) for leading the way to applying scientific methods of Scripture interpretation. Not until Pope Pius XII (Encyclical, Divino Afflante Spiritu) was scientific methodology in interpreting Scripture given the blessing of Roman Catholicism. The Second Vatican Council went a step further and declared that the analysis and synthesis of new theological understanding in the light of evolutionary sense is a "matter as important as can be." (Constitution IV, Gaudium et spes, Introduction, No 4).

The Genesis Creation Myth should be appreciated for what it is — the insight of another time, another worldview. The Old Testament Creation Myth of Genesis isn't adequate for every time because it doesn't credibly inform evolving insights. A theme of cultural belief and political purpose persists in all genres of Old Testament writings, what is the presumption of patriarchal primacy and dominion culture. Women and nature together suffer common exploitation under this blighted male prejudice. Enlightened divinity consciousness opens to the equal-minded roles of females and males in evolving life. To ignore scientific consensus is to imperil ourselves in the blind culture of authoritarian fantasy, arrogant idolatry, and calculated alienation.

ET Item 5: Process Theology

Evolution Theology (ET) has two aspects. The first: like any other field of intelligent inquiry, new insights enter the field and enlarge it in breadth and depth. The second aspect is the fact that Evolution Theology is now developed to the point that it is a field of intelligence and discourse in its own right, because it contains proven self-enlightenment in Divinity Consciousness.

Divinity consciousness is the cumulative body of human insight concerning the "outsideness" of human existence and knowledge, whose content continues to enlarge based on changing contexts and experience. The concept of Trinity, for example, is found in the experience of advanced life forms and basic social structures, including human, that exist as the "thirdness" continuity of parental twoness — father/ mother/ child — family, social unit.

Except for openness of theology to ongoing enlargement, culture loses meaning and effectiveness. For example, Trinity, the threesome consciousness of God, has become dogma-fixated in a way that imprisons divinity in static categories. If however, Trinity is understood more as process than fixed category, human insights can continue to enlarge on Divinity Consciousness in context of open experience.

Godtalkonline keeps open the process of evolving theology by way of enlarging the experience of open WORD-LIGHT-LOVE, categories of Divinity Consciousness, and integrating open experience in the relatedness of the Godly, the natural and the human. Process Theology is inclusive, not exclusive. Everyone participates in the process, in the act of knowledge integration.

ET Item 6: To Evolutionize Theology, not Revolutionize

Better to evolutionize faith and reason than to revolutionize. Non-violence and gradual growth into change are associated with evolution; revolution implies the failure of evolution. What results from failed evolution is maladjustment that happens when consciousness is fixated in cultural dogma that has lost its credibility. The correction of failed evolution and cultural maladjustment causes upheavals and violent revolution. Eucharistic Altruism, as exemplified by Jesus, the Cosmic Christ, is the spiritual insight that renews the symbiotic purpose of every generation.

ET Item7: Equality of Persons

Human beings in common are agents and outcomes of evolution. This is true also in terms of being "religious" agents and outcomes.

As a distinction of interpersonal relationship, religion pertains to moral sense and responsibility. Just as the word religion roots in two (Latin) words, religere (to read, study) and religare (to bind, oblige), and supposes intelligence and obligation, so the distinction of interpersonal relationship supposes intelligence and obligation, gift and task.

"Doing" religion like "doing" theology is equally the prerogative and obligation of every person. Institutions (churches) "do" religion and theology "secondarily;" individual persons do them "primarily."

Evolution Theology is about owning religious intelligence and obligating moral relationship, not letting them be subsumed by institutions but authenticating institutions by maintaining personal ownership of them.

ET Item 8: Public Domain Theology

Creative thinking/ writing belong not just to the individual thinker/ writer, but to the Cosmic well of insights transmitted from generation to generation. All humanity, all life subsists in the Amniotic Water of Cosmic Authenticity. While there are conventional claims of copyright, they should work to stimulate creativity, not stifle it. For this reason, the godtalkonline writings here are meant to be open, for discussion and use, in religious/ civil circles.

ET Item 9: COSMIC SACRAMENT

Experience and self-reflection tell us we have an "inside" and an "outside." The (sacred) remembrance of experience and self-reflection inform us that Cosmic Sacrament (sacred remembrance) is about "insideness" (soul, energy) and "outsideness" (matter, form) — we can't have one without the other! Together, insideness and outsideness are the "selfness" of divine/ human understanding, the work and consciousness of Evolution Theology.

We arrive at understanding only gradually, as individuals and society. The process of gradual understanding is the process of evolution, of entering into the graced Wisdom of Divine Intelligence in the Order of Sacred Remembrance, otherwise called SACRAMENT. Intelligent design is the unfolding Word/ Work of evolution, of theological consciousness.

ET Item 10: Inside Reality's Outside

Everyone generally recognizes that the knowledge of a child is shallower and narrower than an adult's; which observation speaks to the evolution of consciousness. Growth in "grace, age and wisdom" is evolution, personally and collectively. Awakening to evolution is the gradual enlightenment of age, grace and wisdom. But, as with other things new, first, people ignore them, then fight them, and ultimately reject or accept them. Blindness to evolving outsideness deepens the darkness of insideness. We cannot live adult lives if we live closeted in childish understandings.

ET Item 11: What God is About

God is about the insideness and outsideness of being/ becoming. Outsideness is about substance, sensible reality, and insideness is about energy/ spirit, the dynamic that sustains outsideness. There is insideness and outsideness to all substance, what is the exterior "sign" of interior "grace" — Cosmic Sacrament. Evolution is the transformational processing of Cosmic Sacrament, growth in grace, age and wisdom.

Evolution plumbs the depths of potentials and expands the graces of Natural/ Cosmic Sacrament; it liberates consciousness from fixation in limited categories, unlike what institutional religions do in self-interest. Consciousness of other-interest takes one outside limits of self-interest — what "intelligent design" requires. Evolution Theology is about discovering the insideness and outsideness of all existences and accommodating consciousness to the unity and continuity of cosmic reality.

ET Item 12: Call to Community

Meditation is reflection on the insideness of self and other. Self-reflection puts us in touch with divinity, higher spirituality, with the soul of community, that is, with the altruism of otherness and other-concern. The obsession of self-with-self separates one from the allness of other and alienates one from the effective working of divinity. Obsession is fixation in smallness, aloneness and separation.

If we make ourselves islands unto ourselves, we find ourselves in the barrenness of intentional aloneness. We are to be approachable as God is approachable. There is a universality about religion that calls us to community; compassion is the feminine power of insideness. Woman power is the power of love, the better side of otherness, of intentional purpose, the mind and grace of Sacrament, evolution's Sacred Remembrance. The feminine face of community is the inclusive conscience of compassionate love.

ET Item 13: SELF as Sign and Grace

Einstein gives us the science that reveals the joined identity of energy/ matter, spirit/ substance, soul/ body. The conventional (religious) culture of dualism, to the contrary, sets the spiritual and material, soul and body in opposition to each other.

The theology of dualism is a theology that establishes a fundamental distrust between seemingly opposing realms; the presumption of disconnection and opposition self-corrupts for it disconnects from understanding the personal, essential co-identity and mutuality of energy/ matter, spirit/ substance, and soul/ body.

In the transmission of the Garden of Eden Story, males presume themselves to be more Godlike than females for being primary, i.e., directly created by God, whereas, females are male-derived (from Adam's rib); on presumption of direct creation, males presume to have greater "incorruptibility" than females.

Einstein's Special Theory of Relativity, $E=MC^2$, states the equivalency of energy/ matter in every aspect of cosmic characterization. All substance, living and non-living, is energy quantitatively disposed. The specific disposition of substance is also the specific disposition of energy. Specific disposition qualifies energy and matter in apt and sustainable correlations. [The disposition of energy in a bug is different than the disposition of energy in a rock.] The human person, in body characterization, specifies the "Sign" of substance and the "Grace" of energy (spirit) — what is Sacramental Selfhood.

ET Item 14: GRACE as Soul Efficiency

Self-consciously we are aware that we are grace to each other. Grace is religious exchange between persons, what is life's "symbiotic means."

Co-efficiency, the symbiotic working of grace, is a phenomenon of self-and-other consciousness, Einstein's "Celeritas" (C) coefficient. Because of their evolved accommodations, living organisms can interact and appreciate each other. Because of talent of analytical appreciation human beings have the capacity of self-reflection, distinguishing what is symbiotic, what conflicts and disintegrates.

Sense of purpose is morally imagined in consciousness because of the self-reflective capacity of judging what is symbiotic (sustainable) and what isn't. Purpose is a grace of consciousness that directs the trajectory of consciousness in anticipation of future outcomes. Purpose is an "arrow in time;" in aiming its trajectory we know that we "fall short" the target; but the experience of falling-short is the root-consciousness of original sin, the trial-and-error experience of evolution.

ET Item 15: Creative Ambiguity, Electric Surprise

Human experience is ambiguous; it has outcomes in degrees of goodness. It is in the spectrum of goodness that choice is both gift and task; gift, because conscience opens up to the compounding of goodness, and task, because what's perceived as good may not be good; case in point: the presumption of dogma.

The crack between good and lesser good is the window that opens to creativity, the break in continuity that opens a path to new and unpredictable creativity. The old must die to make room for the birth of the new.

Symbiosis evolves in mixed currents of DNA in which micro-organic pathogens may be tamed in unexpected ways, e.g., in which once strange DNA may become compatible. How else explain chlorophyll, the DNA of plastids and mitochondria — the organic complexes responsible for and the dynamics of photosynthesis, anabolism, catabolism and metabolism in cell structuring?

Electricity confounds the intuition that might expect like electrical charges to attract like charges. Well, it works the other way around: in the spectrum of electromagnetism, positive electrical charge attracts negative electrical charge, and, negative charge opposes negative charge, positive charge opposes positive charge. And who would suspect that polarity in cells converges at the equator in emergent organic activity, not unlike planet Earth?

The pattern in cells of "reconciling" opposites is informative in the reconciliation of societal conflicts. Opposing insights should not be dismissed out-of-hand. Escape into clouds of like-mindedness may salve comfort zones of complacency but it is unproductive. Differences in insight need to be embraced as the "crack" in the window of consciousness that opens ambiguity to creative magic.

ET Item 16: Theology is "Word Unlimited"

The Scriptural Canon of Theology is no closed book — which means to say that each generation adds the truth of its learning to the Revelation of Word — Evolution Theology. If the evolution of consciousness is real, then, consciousness continues ever-in-process of finding in its generational newness the meanings that uplift the brought-forward wisdom of prior generations.

And in whom does the experience of newness happen? generally speaking, in everybody. Consciousness includes the deep deposits of intuition attached as "memes" in the codes of DNA. Consciousness is the deposit of wisdom existing in the collective consciousness of the whole people.

The changing experience of the time is the subject matter of conversation in every time. It is the wisdom of the past engaged with the experience of the present that composes evolved theology today — adding generationally to the Canon of Scriptural Revelation. Change is the common element of evolution, experience and consciousness. The collective commentary on change, the "signs of the times," is the stuff of new "truth" revelation. Another word for change is Eucharist, the perpetual transformation of new truth, of Word, made flesh. Divinity is Truth; Truth is Divinity Consciousness. Truth is expressed in Word. Word is unlimited. Seek in the light of your personal consciousness the renewed consciousness of Divinity.

AFTERWORD

The GOSPEL TRUST

The Meaning and the Mystery

The Mysteries of the Rosary, for example, take us on a journey into the lives of Jesus and Mary, recalling the most meaningful and remarkable events in one's own life. Every human life, in some way or other, is an iteration of the mystery and meaning in all life preceding us. The focus of all complexity in human life and in Divine Instance is expressed in the Pieta as perhaps in no other art form. The deep mystery of woman-man, of the divine-natural is essentially represented in the Pieta, the Beatrix Femina.

The missionary/priest/sculptor Peter Weyland, SVD, takes us into life's mystery and meaning, and challenges us to a personal response. The challenge begins in the awareness of universal maternal relationship and the Good News Mission, so poignantly depicted in the "Mater Evangelii Praeconum."

The Good News Gospel is personalized in the life and teaching of Jesus, the Cosmic Christ, whose physical life on Earth has apparently just ended, and which is an obvious agony of consciousness occupying Mary in the moment.

Between the Gospel, the Mother and Jesus, and the observer is consciousness of the challenge of mission, which imposes on the conscience of every Christian, every person, in every age. The breach of the God-Land-Man Trust cannot be resolved except the breach of the God-Woman-Man Trust is also, and firstly, resolved. The waste of nature and the alienation/ exploitation of women are of a piece — both are breaches of the God-Land-Human-Trust.

The Second Coming of the Cosmic Christ in newborn consciousness is frustrated by cultural breaches of Covenant; nature is ever open to new beginnings, but human consciousness is slow in realizing.

Second Coming consciousness imposes personally on every newborn, on each of us personally in the way we live the Gospel Covenant in imitation of the Cosmic Christ, and as transmitted to us by the "Mother of Heralds of the Gospel."

The "Marian" re-presents the divine feminine in the Sacrament of Natural Order. As the Mother of Jesus, who is the Good News, Mary is the Mater Evangelii, the Mother of the Gospel; she is also Mater Praeconum, the Mother of heralds of the Gospel. Each newborn is a wisdom person Second Coming. Between mother and child, Eucharist is the intuitional connection of Word-made-Flesh.

Post Script

Whither the "Catholic" Future? If the Roman Catholic Church can expunge the grievous fault of imperialism from its ecclesial hegemony, it can become the Eucharistic Catholic Church. While I expect the change to happen, I do not expect it to happen in my lifetime. The great and general unsettling amongst denominational Christian churches points to change in the offing.

I envision the direction Catholicism may take, and which I believe the Cosmic Christian vision requires. [Let me again acknowledge that the opinion here is merely that of one of many extra-institutional types.] There is a hunger and desire of a growing body of non-institutional types who see a greater coming together, for amongst the people is the conscious need of convergence more than divergence. One can see beyond institutions and still work with and for institutional redemption.

The common cause of healing the irreligious hurt of global ecology compels all people to be more honest as to institutional complicity in wasting nature. The common, high risk future of life on Earth, perhaps more than anything else, brings people of faith to search for Eucharistic commonality. Fideistic Christian cults will diminish in the face of evolving intelligence — Wisdom.

"Evolution" will be a welcome word, not a feared and demeaned word. Evolution Theology will be valued for its agency in bringing about greater convergence; for reasons of self-interest, even cultic Christians may opt for greater convergence within the vision of Evolution Theology; the Common Cause Movement grounds in knowledge of Eucharistic necessity, physical and psychical.

Recognition of the Instance of Divinity in the Sacrament of Natural Order is a centering attraction, not a backward, but a future-directed trajectory — not just for believers, but for all humanity, all life. The communal future destines all for growth into "otherness," what is growth of realism in a Eucharistic future. The baptismal anointing of universal priesthood will gain in the valuation of faith confirmation. Hierarchical cults of male dominion will be exposed for the injury they have inflicted, and still inflict. Priesthood in the Eucharistic Catholic Church will be recognized in the Baptismal Commission.

The Theology of Trinity (process and Community) will broaden and deepen understanding, and the call for con-celebration will be heard. Authentic compassion will be the root spirituality of and the common impetus for greater Godliness in daily living. The leadership of Eucharistic ecumenism will be led by women, but men will come to recognize common likeness in God. The future promise is the Eucharistic Catholic Church, liberated from Rome.

CONCLUSION

What is Mysticism?

The Cosmic Christ — Divine Instance

With God and nature, women suffer the Good News of ascendant consciousness. Wrapped in the mantle of Divinity humankind cannot escape the insideness of God. God is within. God is above. God is below. God is forward. God is alongside. God is behind. God is breath. God is Life.

Human experience is in and of Divinity. Personhood is the experience of Divinity, of Breath inspiring self-awareness. Consciousness of Presence is Divine Breath informing one and all in Divine Allness. Though in the Presence of God, we are not God, we are the harmony of Divinity in the matter of Cosmic nature. Each of us matters, personally. Because we matter personally, we matter communally, for we are inside each other, intended in/ by the Sacrament of Natural Order to be conscious reminders of the Allness of God.

WORD UNLIMITED — Scripture Unlimited

In the Beginning was The WORD

And The WORD was with God; the WORD is God;

Be it done unto me according to Thy WORD;

And The WORD IS made FLESH; and dwells amongst us;

This Bread, this Wine, is My Body, My Blood

— Do This WORD/ WORK in Memory of Me —

EUCHARIST is Consciousness — Divinely Human

WORD UNLIMITED, WORD out-poured —

Divine Presence — SOPHIA — is Intuitional Wisdom Word-inherited in the Waters of Amniotic Consciousness.

PROGNOSTICATING HISTORY

Before the limitedness of the old can be redeemed in the limitlessness of the new, the old must give itself over for reconciliation in the new. The old must die for the new to be born. History may link the radical diminishment of respect for Roman Catholicism to the Vatican's mean-spirited investigation (Visitation) of the (LCWR), the Leadership Conference of Women Religious; the vacuity of authoritarianism exposes self-alienation in this radical male miscalculation.

In light of this exposure, the insanity of male imperial theology needs to be made accountable to the sanity of divine/ human hypostasis. Divinity Consciousness is equally female/ male. In the scenario of the present time, the imperial "religious right" is in frantic display of hitching its wagon to the political right. This is not a place where YAHWEH, the Compassionate God is found. It is with all humankind that we are both/ and, catholic and Catholic, i.e., cosmic but cult-prone.

Strength, truth and beauty abound in the cosmic universe; servitude and fixity abide in cult. Creativity expands on fractal originality — the common link to God/ Land/ Life, to Earth's diverse complexity. What is complexity? Like the harmonies of music and other sense resonances, complexity is creative amplification on themes of fractal iterations.

"Beauty is truth, truth beauty, —that is all

Ye know on earth and all ye need to know."

(Keats, "Ode on a Grecian Urn")

About the Author

The mission focus and spirituality of the author come naturally to him from family upbringing and educational experience. In his early years the religious atmosphere of family was palpable day-in, day-out, year-in, year-out, including daily Mass, daily rosary, mealtime prayers, morning, and night-time prayers. His eleven years with the Society of the Divine Word imprinted in him the special charism of the SVD and the spirituality of the Divine Word and Holy Spirit.

The mix of Liberal Arts study and habits of spiritual exercises blended in him a balanced sensitivity for the natural and the spiritual. In his Philosophy years the conflicted relationship of faith and reason in church practice troubled him especially, and ultimately led him to the decision to discontinue pursuit of the priesthood in the Roman Catholic Church and the discipline of living in religious community in the Society of the Divine Word.

The spirituality of Divine Word Theology is presented most compellingly in this the 10th book — the "Book End" of his nine "Evolution Trilogies".

http://bookstore.authorhouse.com/AdvancedSearch/Default. aspx?SearchTerm=Sylvester%20L%20Steffen

The Second Enlightenment Trilogy:

PRIMARY SCRIPTURE, Cosmic Religion's First Lessons

QUANTUM RELIGION, the Good News of Rising Consciousness

RELIGION & CIVILITY, the Primacy of Conscience

The Conscious Light Trilogy

THE POSSIBLE JOURNEY, Uncompromised Trust

THE GLOBAL THINKING COMMUNITY, One Family, One Future

GREEN RELIGION, Inside the Cultural Spectrum

The Justified Living Trilogy

2000 SUMMARY PREVISION, Toward Global Revitalization

WHAT SELF DONATION IS, Kenosis, Eucharist & Green Religion

THE POETREE WORLDVIEW, Leafing through History

The Realm of the Infinite Divine: You the reader and I the writer are to each other question and answer. What is our common asking? What is our common answer? Both, answer and question are writ large in our hearts; there, is a grandiose void welling and a grandiose voice swelling that both answers and fulfills. We are a paradox to ourselves. We wonder how we are, how the greatness of soul and the power of grandiosity relate to each other?

Pretense and truth at times are indistinguishable. What is the pretense that drives deception? What is the truth that opens reception? Pretense in its grandiosity is vacuous, whereas, truth in its enlargement is vitalizing. The pretenses of power deceive the soul; the truths of soul dissolve pretenses. In our differences we open to each other our likeness. Differences can enlarge likenesses, if we let them. If we use differences to deceive likenesses, we are the losers. It's for us to choose to pursue likenesses or split over differences — the one choice enlarges, the other does violence and entangles our soul in smallness.

The Cosmic Soul of infinite potential is the place and resource of infinite enlargement, of authentic greatness. Greatness of soul is unpretentious and authentic in power, whereas, imaginings of grandiose power confine soul to smallness. Greatness of soul is the deep welling quest; true enlargement of soul is the common task of nature and personal consciousness.

The fulfilled life is the life that over-powers pretense and opens to truth and renewal. Our personal self-deception is that we think the power of dominion and overreach shows greatness of soul; truth is to the contrary, greatness of soul consists in self-identification with the Immense Other — the Altruism of Eucharist. Enlargement of Soul is by way of Eucharist.

All life accesses the infinite largesse of the Cosmic Soul; self-reflection is aware of potentials of self-enlargement in common with the Cosmic Soul. In our present smallness we cannot know the largeness-potential of Self-Reflection. If we believe that "the best is yet to come", then we must know that we are means to the fulfillment of that end — to the enlargement of soul. Trimorphic Resonance is the power of soul that gives entrance to the greatness of Cosmic Potential that alone self-fulfills, and by which we generationally increase the enlargement of soul. What we seek in life is "soulfulness." Our dreams about heaven open us to soulfulness. Desires, dreams and destiny converge, enlarge and emerge. Eucharistic Soul emerges and converges in the Realm of the Infinite Divine by the soulfulness of compassion, in the here and now.

www.divinicom.com

About Peter Weyland, SVD

Peter Weyland was born the 2nd child of 10 children to Nicolas Weyland and Maria Falk, Stacyville, Iowa; baptized on June 2, 1895, at Visitation B.V.M.

Graduated from St. John University, Collegeville, MN; entered the Novitiate of the Society of the Divine Word, September 8, 1915, at Techny, IL; made his profession of perpetual vows on September 8, 1919; was ordained to the Priesthood on May 1, 1921, one of the first three priests to be ordained at Techny.

His first mission was to the Philippines in April, 1922; for two years in Manila, he was prefect of students at St. Rita's Residence Hall. In 1925, he returned to Techny and taught Latin for three years; after which he pursued art study at the Pennsylvania Academy of Fine Arts; with some disruption he completed his art study and returned to Techny to teach; he served as chaplain to the Sisters of the Holy Spirit of Perpetual Adoration (Pink Sisters) of the Convent of Divine Love in Philadelphia. In 1941 he supervised the opening of the new seminary at Bordentown, New Jersey. He returned to Techny, August 1942, where he taught academic courses and served as rector, 1943 – 1946. After 1949 he continued to teach, and set up his loft studio in one of the Techny towers.

In preparation for sculpting the Pieta he suspended himself 31 times for 30 minutes each time from a cross while students made plaster casts of his body. From his research he was convinced that Jesus' body would have been rigid from rigor mortis; he sculpted the corpus of the Pieta in the rigor position. From his research and study of the Shroud of Turin he authored the book "A Sculptor Interprets the Holy Shroud," copyright 1954, Mission Press, Techny, IL.

Courtesy of the Robert M. Myers Archives, Techny, IL

Arnold Steffen, SVD, missionary priest to Papua New Guinea since 1957 to the present time (2011), a student of Father Weyland, offered this: "Peter Weyland -- born, 02.06.1895, reared Stacyville, IA, died at Techny, 20.05.1969. Taught at Techny, including in my time Sacred Art, Homiletics, had his art studio in a tower at Techny, where he also simulated crucifixion to study muscular tensions to guide his representations. In homiletics he taught us we had to make ourselves heard to avoid wasting our own and congregations' time. He was a big 'refrigerator-build' of a man with voice to match. Like our father, of Luxembourg ancestry.

SVD Presence in NE Iowa

The mission of bringing awarenesss of the SVD to Northeast Iowa owes much to a one time mariner on the flagship HOHNEZOLLERN of Kaiser Wilhelm, one Peter John Naebers; born January 3, 1866, at Aldekirk, Krei Geldern, Niederskrein, Germany. His parents were Pater John Naebers and Margaret Luern Naebers.

In his youth, Peter Naebers studied at religious houses in Germany and also at St. Michaels's Mission House, Steyl, Holland, under the direction of Father Arnold Janssen, S.V.D., founder of the Society the Divine Word. Peter promised Father Janssen that he would spend his life doing good for the Mission Society and bring as many young men to it as he could. He kept his promise, and through his direct influence he fostered vocations for the Society of the Divine Word. "It was through Father Naebers that so many fine young men from the Barclay Parish joined the Society." [See reference below]

Peter Naebers was 27 years old when he came to America in 1893. He entered St. Meinrad Seminary, Meinrad, IN, and completed his theology studies. He was ordained to the priesthood at St. Meinrad Seminary on June 13, 1897. He celebrated his First Mass at SS. Peter and Paul Parish Church, Petersburg, IA, where he served until 1899. That same year he was appointed pastor of the Visitation B.V.M. Church at Stacyville, IA. There he supervised the construction of a new Gothic style church.

As the population outgrew the church, Father Naebers proposed and followed through the building of a new church and school at nearby Meyer, IA. The first Mass celebrated at the Meyer, Sacred Heart Church, was in January 1901. Nine years later Father Naebers became pastor of St. Mary Church, Roseville, IA. In 1914, he was appointed pastor of St. Joseph Church, Independence, IA. In 1919, Archbishop Keane appointed Father Naebers pastor of St. Francis Church, Barclay Township, Dunkerton, IA. Here he continued his work of mission until his death on September 15, 1934. His body is entombed in the St. Francis Cemetery, Barclay Parish.

The Society of the Divine Word is the beneficiary of the paternity of Father Naebers in which he labored as a preeminent "herald of the Gospel." Peter Weyland, and the many vocations that came from St. Francis Parish, are blood-connected by family connections, over some seven generations. Such names come to mind, as: Beehner, Delagardelle, Falk, Frost, Hayes, Kass, Koester, Koster, Knebel, Lillig, Magee, McGarvey, Meier, Muehlig, Nuebel, Ortscheid, Penne, Pfiffner, Risse, Sader, Sadler, Schares, Schmitt, Shimp, Steffen, Weber, Wellner, Weyland, Wingert, and many others not listed here.

The mingled blood lines of NE Iowa immigrant families credit the mission and history of the Society of the Divine Word. Names such as: John Koster, Vincent Staebell, Claire Risse, Roger Risse, Donald Ehr, Arnold Steffen, James Risse, and others who pursued studies with the SVD but returned to family living and have kept alive charisms learned from religious and regular studies with the SVD. I am one of the latter privileged.

Reference: detailed documentation, especially of the history of the Barclay, St. Francis Parish, is painstakingly accounted for in the book BARCLAY REVIEWED, By Roy C. Ortner, copyright 1974, Schiller Park, IL. The information above has been excerpted directly from the Roy Ortner book.

Barclay No. 3, c. 1940, Dunkerton, Iowa

Back Row, left to right

Arnold Steffen (SVD), Eleanor Steffen (Sr. M Justina, OSF), Roger Risse (SVD)

Middle row:

Left end, Vincent B. Steffen, former Chickasaw County State Representative and Speaker of the Iowa House; right end, Mrs. Blanch Hogan, teacher

Front row, from right to left:

Elizabeth Naebers, Ralph Steffen, Sylvester Steffen (11-year SVD), James Risse (SVD)

BOOKS by SYLVESTER L STEFFEN

"EDEN'S LIFEWORK POETREE"
— The POETREE Trilogies (1999)
Nine Chapbooks at: www.evolution101.org

I. NOVOGENESIS
1. Word Beginnings
2. The Ground of Faith
3. The Spreading Word

II. METAGENESIS
1. Becoming Consciousness
2. The Ground of Hope
3. Reflective Symbiosis

III. THEOGENESIS
1. Wisdom's Choice
2. (Love's) Disturbed Grounds
3. Personal Conscience
Books End: "The House of Bread, Eucharistic Continuity"

The DIVINICON
(The Evolution Trilogies)

I. The Second Enlightenment Trilogy
1. PRIMARY SCRIPTURE, Cosmic Religion's First Lessons
2. QUANTUM RELIGION, the Good News of Rising Consciousness
3. RELIGION & CIVILITY, the Primacy of Conscience

II. The Conscious Light Trilogy
1. THE POSSIBLE JOURNEY, Uncompromised Trust
2. THE GLOBAL THINKING COMMUNITY, One Family, One Future
3. GREEN RELIGION, Inside the Cultural Spectrum

III. The Justified Living Trilogy
1. 2000 SUMMARY PREVISION, Toward Global Revitalization
2. WHAT SELF DONATION IS, Kenosis, Eucharist & Green Religion
3. THE POETREE WORLDVIEW, Leafing through History
Books End: "WORD UNLIMITED, Divinely Maternal"